THE

PREPPY

COOKBOOK

THE

PREPPY

COOKBOOK

Classic Recipes for the Modern Prep

CHRISTINE E. NUNN

PHOTOGRAPHS BY TED AXELROD
ILLUSTRATIONS BY ASHLEY HALSEY

NEW HARVEST
BOSTON NEW YORK 2013

This book is printed on acid-free paper. ∞

Published by Houghton Mifflin Harcourt Publishing Company, New York, New York.
Published Simultaneously in Canada.
For information about permission to reproduce selections from this book,
write to Permissions, Houghton Mifflin Harcourt Publishing Company,
215 Park Avenue South, New York, New York 10003.

www.hmhbooks.com

For more information about the photographs featured in this book, visit
www.axelrodphotography.com. For the illustrations, visit www.ahalsey.com.

Library of Congress Cataloging-in-Publication Data
Nunn, Christine E.
The preppy cookbook : classic recipes for the modern prep / Christine E. Nunn ;
photographs by Ted Axelrod.
pages cm
Includes index.
ISBN 978-0-544-11458-6
1. Cooking, American. 2. Preppies—Social life and customs. I. Title.
TX715.N95 2013
641'5973—dc23
2013019222

Book design by Elizabeth Van Itallie

Printed in The United States of America
DOC 10 9 8 7 6 5 4 3 2 1

This book is dedicated to the memory of my mom, Carol Anderton Nunn, a class act whose love of food and cooking made me who I am today. And to my dad, Richard C. Nunn, a successful gentleman who was passionate about his garden, enjoyed a good round of golf, and was the kindest soul around.

CONTENTS

FOREWORD

I read *The Official Preppy Handbook* when it came out in 1980 and chuckled along with everyone else, pretending that that lifestyle had nothing to do with me. In fact, a full decade before the book's publication, this rebellious child of the sixties had shed almost all of the obvious affectations that marked her as a prep. On the lunch line during my first week at the University of Michigan in 1970, I made the mistake of asking for a bacon-lettuce-and-*toMAHto* sandwich. The entire cafeteria, students and servers alike, stopped dead and looked at me as if I'd dropped into their midst from another planet. From then on I pronounced that word like everyone around me.

But, hey, those are my roots. Although I grew up in New York City, my parents and all their kin are from solid New England stock, and their forebears from Olde England and Scotland and France. As a kid, I attended private schools, played tennis, attempted to sail, attempted to learn how to ride a horse, visited coastal Maine, summered at my parents' country home in Massachusetts, and traveled throughout Europe after graduating from college. As an adult, I have always been ready for a glass of wine at the stroke of six o'clock.

Like Lisa Birnbach and yours truly, my friend Christine Nunn grew up in the wonderful world of prep. And like Lisa, she writes about that world with deep knowledge and humor. But with *The Preppy Cookbook*, Christine takes *The Official Preppy Handbook* several steps further, deep into the preppy kitchen. It is a place where mayonnaise is The Condiment, gin and tonic is The Drink, a Bloody Mary is The Cure, condensed soup in a can is a mother sauce, Jell-O molds are elegant, and caviar and Champagne are de rigueur on holidays (although only two brands are considered acceptable). It is a cozy, noncombative, well-lubricated world, very reminiscent of Jeeves and Wooster.

I first met Christine in 2006 on a charity cruise in New York Harbor to raise money for multiple sclerosis research. I was the featured chef and Christine and her catering crew had donated food to the event. We hit it off immediately, especially after we discovered that both of us were alums of the Culinary Institute of America.

Several months later, Christine reached out to ask if I would work with her on an event to raise money for a little girl with a terrible heart condition. All I had to do was show up early enough to check on the preparation of my recipes and then attend the dinner. When I arrived at the venue, Christine's first question was, "What would you like for a cocktail?" "Hmmmm," I thought. "It is within spitting distance of 6 p.m. I like this woman."

The next year the James Beard Foundation asked me to prepare salad for three hundred for one of their annual awards dinners. Lacking the resources of a restaurant, including a battalion of sous chefs, I couldn't have done it on my own. Happily, Christine rode to the rescue. She brought her crew and most of the ingredients as well. Everything went swimmingly. Christine is always bailing people out.

But she is a very talented chef, too, as anyone lucky enough to have dined at Picnic, her restaurant in Fair Lawn, New Jersey, can attest. Its occasionally tongue-in-cheek text aside, this cookbook boasts a raft of seriously good recipes and an equal number of great ideas for their presentation. (Watch your back, Martha S.!)

The book is organized to reflect the stations of the Preppy Life Cycle, including The Formative Years, Summer and the Living Is Easy (featuring a Lobster Bake worthy of Julia Child), Brunch as a Verb (hooray for seven varieties of Eggs Benedict!), Luncheons and Showers (including a dozen renditions of the dreaded but ever-popular tea sandwich), and, of course, Home for the Holidays.

The thoughtful and mannerly Ms. Nunn also dispenses prep etiquette at every step. Handwritten thank-you notes are a must. Brunch should begin at 12:15. A shower should never be held at the home of the mother of the bride or of the expectant mother. Do not cheapen your Christmas tree with tinsel or garlands.

Even if you don't smile your way through this book (although I did), and even if you aren't a preppy or preppy wannabe, I'm sure you'll want to prepare many of these dishes—and their accompanying cocktails—for friends and family. All kidding aside, preps are a famously sociable tribe, a tribe that loves to entertain. Welcome to the party.

—Sara Moulton,
host of *Sara's Weeknight Meals*

INTRODUCTION

As I sit on the porch of my little lake house on this late summer day, awaiting the arrival of my weekend guests, I can't help but contemplate how the world has changed to the detriment of gracious living. What happened, I wonder, to the days of a handwritten invitation where the invitee would actually write back? It was a polite world, not too long ago.

The weekend party I am planning is small but fun. We'll start with drinks outside. I'm all set with the makings of martinis, which of course means gin. (Rule one: Vodka is not in a martini unless it is called a vodka martini, which really is not a martini at all. And don't even think that a French martini is French or a martini. It is simply a vodka drink.) We'll move on to some snacks, cheese, crackers, olives (I've got those anyway for the above drink).

Yes, indeedy, the entire weekend will be a party! After cocktails, I'll light the grill, for I have a fun lobster bake planned. I'll have the finger bowls ready, and the food all set to pop on the grill, so that I can join my guests almost the entire time I am cooking. I've picked out three great wines to serve, and the table is already set with shellfish forks and nutcrackers.

For the morning, I have planned a great eye-opener of a breakfast, involving plenty of pork products and eggs. These are key, along with Clamato Bloodies (an appropriate use for vodka), which I'll make from the mix that is already hiding in the back of the fridge. After an afternoon of outdoor activities (including a rousing game of croquet and a canoe trip on the lake), we'll cool down with some cocktails and grill a great porterhouse steak with a few terrific sides. A casual brunch with the neighbors will round out the weekend.

With this party, I'm reviving the good old days of preppy living at its best, and I invite you to join me along the way. The book you hold in your hand offers up the finest way to entertain, live, and eat, with a gin and tonic in hand and decked out in outrageous Lilly Pulitzer prints!

The kitchen is the soul of the preppy household. Wheat Thins, port wine cheese, leftovers, and mixers are always on hand. And the preppy cook has an arsenal of great recipes for all occasions, from dropping off a covered dish to a neighbor to throwing a black-tie party. And, of course, we entertain and dine consistently using proper manners (remember, always pick up your asparagus; never use a fork unless it is smothered in your perfect hollandaise sauce). Just like our style, the food we prepare goes from the most understated to the most outlandish without ever being gaudy. And just as we keep a sweater for twenty years (being frugal means more money to spend on the sailboat), we waste not, want not. Preppies cook just as well as we play tennis, golf, and open Champagne—perhaps even better.

The iconic book of the early eighties, *The Official Preppy Handbook*, let the world know, in no uncertain terms, that one does not have to be white Anglo-Saxon Protestant (WASP) to be a prep. And, for a little while there, people listened.

The Preppy Cookbook will guide you, step by step, in creating a kitchen and a world that personifies the lifestyle we all have a right to live.

From the cure for a Sunday morning hangover to an elegant bridal shower, from casserole to standing rib roast, tailgating, summering, and more, you can rest assured that no matter what the social situation, you will be prepared—and admired—for your good taste.

—Christine E. Nunn

A NOTE ABOUT the RECIPES IN THIS BOOK

Some assumptions for the reader:

Butter is unsalted.

Flour is all-purpose.

Stock is either homemade or low-sodium.

Scant means a tad.

Olive oil is not extra-virgin, unless specified.

Nothing is low-fat or reduced fat.

Mayonnaise is Hellmann's or, for those west of the Mississippi, Best Foods.

Herbs are fresh unless dried is specified.

Onions are Vidalia or another sweet onion.

Fish is fresh, never frozen.

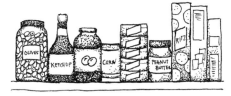

THE

FORMATIVE

YEARS

COMFORT FOODS
AND CASSEROLES

This is the food we first tasted on a silver spoon. On a chilly night, after a long day out at the hunt, in the canoe, or on a brisk hike, nothing beats a nice comforting meal. We preps are a modest folk in many ways. Many of us have simple palates, and sometimes the most straightforward foods give us the most joy. Thinking back to the Boston Brahmins of years ago, of course, meat, potatoes, gravy . . . these are the tastes that run through that very blue blood. Our parents grew up with these recipes, and their parents before them. They are the taste of home.

A strong bread wrapped ... over ...
... from, allowing ends to extend ...
... of pan for easy cake removal.

1 cup of Pillsbury White Cake Mix batter ...
pan back pan. Bake remaining batter ...
... cupcakes. ...

Meringue over batter, smooth with spat...
ula. Sprinkle with mixture of 1 tablespoon
sugar, ½ teaspoon cinnamon, and ½ cup
blanched slivered almonds.

... Bor ... for 25 to 30 minutes until lightly
browned. Place one cooled layer meringue-
side down on serving plate. Spread with
cooked prepared vanilla pudding mix. Top
with second layer, meringue-side up. If
desired, garnish with fresh fruit. Serve ...
10 to 12.

MERINGUE: Beat 4 egg whites until soft mounds ...
Gradually add ½ cup sugar, beating well af...
addition. Continue beating until mering...
stiff, glossy peaks.

... ps sugar
... butter
... milk
... eggs
... baking ...
... ups flour
...lavoring ...
...uit if desire...

Crab dip or chees...
1 8z cr chee...
milk
finely chopp...
horse rad...
blend we...
slivered ...
oven

CREAMED CHIPPED BEEF
ON POTATOES

SERVES 4 GENEROUSLY

Creamed chipped beef on toast was a staple during World War II and went on to become a prep school favorite. While it can still be found throughout our great land, I have only seen it on diner menus in the Philadelphia area. When I see it, I order it. Its rather unsavory nickname is SOS, for "sh★t on a shingle," the shingle being toast. I like it with potatoes, known as SOP, but I think of it as sop, as in sop up all the alcohol from the night before. The recipe calls for dried beef, which is difficult to find sliced to order. Luckily, it comes in nifty little jars that allow it to be kept on hand for years. Our brave soldiers who protected us first ate that beef during World War II. Thanks to them, well, we can have SOP whenever we like or, more importantly, need.

4 tablespoons butter
3 russet potatoes, peeled and thinly
    sliced
½ small white onion, minced
2 tablespoons flour
1 cup whole milk plus ½ cup, if needed

1 cup half-and-half
1 2.5-ounce jar dried beef, shredded,
    soaked in milk for 1 hour, and drained
Pinch of cayenne pepper
Salt and black pepper to taste

For the Potatoes: In a large skillet (preferably cast iron), melt 2 tablespoons of the butter over medium heat. Working in batches, place one layer of potatoes in the skillet. Cover and reduce the heat to low. After about 15 minutes, remove the lid and raise the heat to medium high. Brown the potatoes, turning carefully, about three minutes. Set aside and repeat process until all potatoes are cooked. Depending on the size of your skillet it could be two or three batches in total. Worry not if the potatoes cool while you finish cooking, as the sauce from the chipped beef will warm them immediately.

For the Sh★t: In a large saucepan, melt the remaining butter over medium heat. Add the onion and sweat until soft, about 5 minutes. Add the flour, reduce the heat to very low, and stir slowly, making sure the flour stays a very light yellow color and does not brown, for 10 minutes. (This step is crucial to ensuring the SOP doesn't taste like S from the flour not being cooked properly.)

(continued on following page)

Add 1 cup of the milk, the half-and-half, and the beef, stirring constantly, so that no lumps form, for 10 minutes. (It's better to stir than whisk, as you don't want the beef to get caught up in a whisk.) Add the cayenne, and season with salt and black pepper to taste. If the sauce is too thick, add additional milk to taste, and if there is no hint of flour, it is ready to serve. If there is still a slight flour taste, continue cooking until the sauce is smooth, and velvety.

To serve, place the potatoes on a warmed platter and spoon the sauce over them. Serve the remaining sauce on the side.

Note: Depending on how salty the beef is, you may not need to add any additional salt.

EILEEN'S CRABBIES

MAKES 128 HORS D'OEUVRES

Gosh, this recipe for a cheesy crab appetizer has been around forever. I've seen so many variations of it, but all the cooks' notes always say the same thing: pop them in the freezer and bring them out when you have unexpected company. My dearly departed next-door neighbor at the lake house would make these as soon as she opened the house for the summer. Sure enough, she kept them in the freezer. The fact is, they never stayed there long. She'd come knocking at my door with a paper plate of crabbies, hot out of the toaster oven, and a bottle of wine, and the next thing you knew all the neighbors were over nibbling on these little English muffin classics.

1 pound backfin or "special" crabmeat*
1 cup (2 sticks) butter, softened
2 6-ounce jars cheese spread, such as
    Old English
¼ cup mayonnaise

1 tablespoon lemon juice
1½ tablespoons seasoned salt
1 tablespoon garlic salt
16 English muffins, halved

Pick through the crabmeat and put in a small bowl. In a medium bowl, add the butter, cheese spread, and mayonnaise, and with an electric mixer, beat at medium speed for 4 minutes, or until well combined. Fold in the crab, the lemon juice, seasoned salt, and garlic salt.

Place the muffin halves on a baking sheet and spread the crabmeat mixture evenly on top of them. Freeze for at least 30 minutes. Cut each muffin half in quarters. Portion the crabbies as you please into zipper-lock bags for future use.

To reheat, place the crabbies on a baking sheet or on foil. Toast in the toaster oven at 350°F for about five minutes, or until the cheese is just bubbling. Serve hot.

Note: The crabmeat, found in the seafood section of the grocery store, is a cheaper version than lump crabmeat. It is comprised of the smaller pieces of crabmeat and perfect for crabbies.

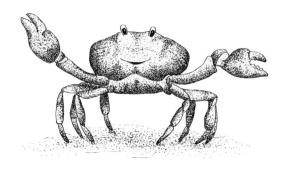

THICK-AS-LONDON-FOG PEA SOUP

MAKES ABOUT HALF A GALLON

There is nothing like a nice big pot of pea soup simmering on the stove on a cold winter afternoon. This soup may be time consuming, taking about two hours of cooking time, but it is well worth the wait. Because you have to stir it so frequently, I usually make it while I am cooking something else so that my time in the kitchen is well spent. The soup keeps well and is even better the second day.

1 medium onion, finely chopped	9 cups chicken stock
2 tablespoons butter	1 ham hock
1 1-pound bag split peas, picked through and rinsed	4 bay leaves
2 carrots, finely sliced	Salt and pepper to taste

In a large stockpot over medium heat, sweat the onion in the butter for about 5 minutes. Add the split peas and carrots, and cover with 6 cups of stock. Add the ham hock and bay leaves.

Bring the soup to a boil over medium high heat. Reduce the heat to low and simmer, uncovered, for about 2 hours. Stir frequently, making sure to scrape the bottom of the pot, adding more stock as needed. The soup should be quite thick. As the split peas and carrots break down, use the back of a spoon to squash the carrots into the soup. Continue cooking until the peas and carrots are completely broken down and the soup is thick.

Remove the ham hock, peel off the skin. Shred any meat on it, and return the meat to the soup. Discard the skin and bone and the bay leaves.

Taste and season with salt and pepper if desired. (Do not add salt before tasting; depending on your chicken stock and ham hock, you may not need it.)

Serve in a deep soup bowl or mug.

ZUCCHINI PIE

MAKES ONE 9-INCH PIE

When the zucchini from the garden were in full season and we could not give them away, my parents found a way to serve them every single day, or so it felt. Zucchini bread, pancakes, casseroles, you name it. But this zucchini pie was, gad-zukes, my favorite. A variation of the Bisquick "Impossible Pie" recipe, it is comfort in a slice, and with all those veggies, it's pretty good for you too!

3 cups shredded zucchini
½ cup grated onion
½ cup grated Parmesan or cheddar
   cheese

1 garlic clove, finely chopped
½ cup vegetable oil
4 eggs, beaten
1 cup Bisquick or other quick biscuit mix

Preheat the oven to 350°F. Grease a 9-inch deep-dish pie plate.

In a large bowl, mix the zucchini, onion, cheese, garlic, oil, eggs, and Bisquick until incorporated.

Pour the zucchini mixture into the prepared pie plate.

Bake for 35 to 40 minutes, or until set.

Can be served immediately. It is still yummy when cool.

DIRTY GIRL SCOUT

A Dirty Girl Scout gets its name from the color of the drink, which looks to be the same as a vintage uniform and tastes just like a Thin Mint cookie. It is not terribly preppy and is a recent addition to our beverage repertoire. However, because it tastes like childhood and provides a fun buzz, it can be included.

1 fluid ounce Baileys Irish Cream
½ fluid ounce vodka
1 fluid ounce Kahlúa

½ fluid ounce green crème de menthe
1 Thin Mint cookie, crumbled

Fill a highball glass halfway with ice cubes. Add the Baileys, vodka, and Kahlúa. Stir. Pour the crème de menthe in the center of the drink to create the look of the Girl Scout uniform. Garnish with the crumbled Thin Mint.

CONDENSED SOUP AS A MOTHER SAUCE

Sometimes there is no greater joy in life than dressing up in your finest St. John dress and heading out for a night on the town. Other days, there is nothing as comforting as donning an old polo shirt and pair of shorts, eating chips and dip, and playing cards with friends. Well, the same holds true at the dinner table.

Many great recipes start with the classic French "mother sauces." These five sauces are the cornerstone for most classic French dishes. Hollandaise is one, and another, béchamel, is often used in the preppy repertoire, with great dishes such as mac and cheese and SOP. Espagnole, velouté, and tomato round out the mother sauces. All well and good, that, but really, who on a regular basis is going to go to the trouble of making those sauces except if cooking for a showstopping occasion? Not me.

I am pretty darned sure though that everybody has a can of condensed soup sitting in a cabinet. I sure do, and I know for sure it is *the* mother sauce of many a great dish. The basis of some of the most beloved dishes in a preppy's cooking arsenal are cream of mushroom, cheddar cheese, tomato, cream of chicken, or, if you are really feeling fancy, cream of asparagus.

Condensed soups provide endless possibilities for fast dinners that are simple, heartwarming, and as classic as roasted tenderloin of beef.

A FEW EXAMPLES:

- Add some milk, some Worcestershire sauce, a bit of shredded cheddar cheese, and some beer to cheddar cheese soup, slap it over toast and you have a swell Welsh rarebit.

- Cream of broccoli soup, some mayo, some milk, and cheddar cheese mixed in with a bag of frozen broccoli makes a great broccoli cheddar dish suitable for any preppy dinner table. Feel free to sub or include cauliflower in that mix. Top it with buttered bread crumbs. Who could resist?

- Some pork chops, apple cider vinegar, brown sugar, a chopped onion, and tomato soup makes for a great baked "barbecue" pork dinner. Prep time? About as long as it takes to mix the first drink of the evening.

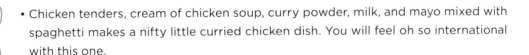

- Chicken tenders, cream of chicken soup, curry powder, milk, and mayo mixed with spaghetti makes a nifty little curried chicken dish. You will feel oh so international with this one.

- Who doesn't really love a good tuna noodle casserole? And what is the sauce that binds this together? Cream of mushroom soup, of course. Just add the soup, the canned tuna, some cooked spaghetti, mayo, and milk.

- Thinly sliced corned beef, a can of sauerkraut, Swiss cheese, rye bread, egg noodles, and Thousand Island dressing, all mixed up with cream of chicken soup makes a great Reuben casserole. It is a nice frugal way to use up St. Paddy's Day leftovers. (Yes, we preps can celebrate St. Paddy's. I'm quite sure the Kennedys do.)

- What Thanksgiving table is complete without green bean casserole? A simple version can be assembled in about five minutes with dried fried onions, cream of mushroom soup, milk, mayo, green beans, and a drop of Worcestershire sauce.

Most of these dishes only require a casserole dish, some type of noodle or rice to soak up the extra sauce, and to be baked in a 350°F oven for about 20 minutes. The fact is, making any of these dishes will warm the cockles of any preppy's soul because it is comfort food that really tastes like childhood and home. Not only that, it shows that, really, one frequently has much better things to worry about than making a fancy meal.

BAKED HAM STEAK WITH PINEAPPLE AND MAPLE GLAZE

SERVES 6 GOOD EATERS, WITH A BIT OF LEFTOVERS FOR BREAKFAST

Oh, poor ham steak, you have been forgotten in the pantheon of proteins! Perhaps it is your sodium content? Perhaps you are just too simple to cook? Perhaps your agreeable price makes you too pedestrian for most palates? Well, dear ham steak, you will always have a place in my heart and my recipe collection.

Ham steak makes a really quick, really easy dinner. Thank goodness, over the years, the sodium content has dropped significantly. I almost always have one in my fridge as a culinary equivalent of a security blanket. It has a really long shelf life if unopened, so if the cupboard is bare, dinner is still there. Additionally, if I have a hankering for eggs but don't have any bacon, well, I can fry up a little piece of ham steak in about four minutes.

2 18-ounce ham steaks
½ cup packed light brown sugar
1 8-ounce can pineapple slices, drained
   with juice reserved

1 8-ounce can diced pineapple, drained
   with juice reserved
3 tablespoons maple syrup
1 tablespoon butter

Preheat the oven to 350°F.

Place one ham steak in a 9 x 13-inch Pyrex baking dish. Stack the remaining ham steak evenly over the first ham steak. Sprinkle with ¼ cup of the brown sugar. Top with the juice from the pineapple slices and the pineapple slices.

Bake, uncovered, for 15 to 20 minutes, until warmed through.

Transfer the ham steaks to a warm platter, keeping the pineapple on top. Cover loosely with foil.

Transfer the juice from the baking dish to a small saucepan. Add the diced pineapple with its juice, the remaining ¼ cup brown sugar, the maple syrup, and butter. Bring to a boil over high heat. Reduce the heat to low and simmer for 10 minutes, until slightly thickened.

Pour half of the glaze over the ham steak, serving any remaining glaze on the side.

CORN FRITTERS

MAKES 8-10 FRITTERS

I'm not a fan of frozen or canned corn, but when corn is out of season and you have a craving for it, a good fritter hides the fact that the corn is, well, not fresh. Fritters make for a tasty side dish that works swimmingly with the Baked Ham Steak with Pineapple and Maple Glaze (page 27).

1 egg, beaten
¼ cup whole milk
¾ cup flour
1 teaspoon baking powder
2 teaspoons sugar

¾ teaspoon salt
Dash of pepper
1 cup canned or cooked frozen corn
¼ cup vegetable or corn oil

In a small bowl, combine the egg and milk. In a large bowl, sift the flour, baking powder, sugar, salt, and pepper. Add the egg-milk mixture to the flour mixture and stir until combined. Fold in the corn.

Heat a griddle until it's good and hot, and add the oil.

Working in batches, drop the corn mixture by the spoonful onto the griddle. Cook for 2 minutes on each side, or until golden brown.

Drain on paper towels. Serve immediately.

BRAISE ONE, BRAISE THEM ALL

Braising produces the most comforting of comfort foods. The house smells great, the kitchen is warm and inviting, and usually the food is laden with gravy, aromatic vegetables, and melt-in-your-mouth meat. Once you master the standard procedure for braising, you can experiment and create your own wonderful meals. The easiest way to start is with pot roast (page 30). The method of browning the meat, adding vegetables and tomato paste, making a simple roux, and then deglazing the pan is the start to almost every braise.

One of the nicest things about braising is that you can use whichever vegetables you like. Love potatoes? Add more. Hate carrots? Don't use them. However, if you want to add vegetables that are not firm root vegetables or tubers, such as green beans or broccoli, add them much later in the cooking process or you will wind up with a brown, overly cooked mess.

GREAT CUTS OF MEAT TO BRAISE, WITH SOME SEASONING IDEAS

• Pork shoulder, with pearl onions, barbecue seasonings, and cubes of bacon

• Lamb shanks with Madras curry powder, cumin, parsnips, raisins, and figs

• Veal shanks with orange juice, tomatoes, white wine, and mushrooms

• Pork shanks with apple cider, apples, onions, and turnips with a few cloves thrown in

• Beef brisket with chile sauce, Coca-Cola, carrots, and instant onion soup mix

PERFECT POT ROAST

SERVES 6 WITH SOME LEFTOVERS FOR SANDWICHES

There is nothing like the smell of a house on a late-autumn Sunday afternoon when a pot roast is slowly cooking in a Dutch oven. It's a simple one-pot dinner, which I adore, because who really wants to spend the afternoon cleaning up? While it slowly cooks, you can do something more important, like watch the football game. I don't think there is a much better lunch than a hot, open-faced pot roast sandwich made with the leftovers!

Ask the butcher to leave a bit of the fat on, it will melt in and give more flavor and moistness to the finished roast

Flour for dredging
1 teaspoon salt
1 teaspoon pepper
1 5- to 7-pound beef roast, such as rump roast (my preference), eye round, or bottom round
¼ cup vegetable oil
8 carrots, cut into 2-inch slices

3 stalks celery, cut into 2-inch dice
2 medium onions, quartered
2 tablespoons tomato paste
3 cups beef stock, plus more as needed
2 bay leaves
2 sprigs fresh thyme
8 red potatoes, quartered
1 tablespoon butter

Preheat the oven to 325°F.

On a plate, mix together the flour, salt, and pepper. Generously dredge the roast in the seasoned flour, turning to coat all sides. The extra flour mixed with the olive oil will create a roux.

In a heavy Dutch oven large enough to fit the roast, heat the oil over medium-high heat. When the pan is good and hot, add the roast and sear for 2 to 3 minutes on all sides, adjusting the heat as needed so the flour does not burn. Transfer the roast to a large platter.

Reduce the heat to medium low and add the carrots, celery, and onions and sauté until slightly cooked, about 5 minutes. Add the tomato paste and cook until the paste turns a rust color, about 5 minutes, constantly scraping the bottom of the pan to get any of the remaining brown bits from the roast. Return the roast, fat side up, and its juices to the pan and pour the stock over it. Add the bay leaves and thyme. Cover, and place in the oven for 2 hours.

Turn the roast over and check to make sure that the liquid is halfway up the sides of the roast. If not, add more stock as needed. Return the pot to the oven and cook 1 hour more, then add potatoes to the pot and cook another hour.

Transfer the roast to a platter and cover tightly with foil. Let rest at least 20 minutes.

While the roast rests, discard the bay leaves and thyme. Bring the sauce and veggies to a boil over high heat and cook for about 10 minutes, until it has thickened enough to

coat a wooden spoon. With a slotted spoon, transfer half the veggies and half the sauce to a blender. Blend on low for 2 minutes, or until the mixture forms a very thick sauce. Pour the sauce back into pot, and stir to blend with the veggies. Swirl in the butter until melted.

Carve the roast against the grain in ¼-inch slices and serve with veggie-laden sauce.

CLASSIC MEAT LOAF

SERVES 6

By gosh, by golly, meat loaf may be the most all-American of main dishes. Blue plate special, for sure, but my inner child wants meat loaf when the going gets tough. And I love it even more the next day, cold on a sandwich with mayo and ketchup.

The trick to my meat loaf is that I cook it on slices of white bread (thanks for the hint, Sara Moulton). The bread removes a lot of the fat from the pan and forms a nice crust on the bottom. Use as many slices of white bread that your personally shaped meat loaf needs. I used to cook it in a loaf pan, but found that made for a greasy loaf. Now, I cook it in a Pyrex baking dish, and the end result shows that it works very well—crusty on the outside and moist on the inside.

3 tablespoons butter
1 large onion, diced
3 stalks celery, diced
2 cups cubed seasoned stuffing bread
⅔ cup whole milk
3 pounds ground beef or meat loaf mix
(veal, pork, and beef)

5 dashes of Maggi sauce
1 egg, beaten
3 tablespoons tomato paste
1 teaspoon salt
1 teaspoon pepper
2 or 3 slices firm white bread

Preheat the oven to 350°F.

In a large sauté pan, melt the butter over low heat. Add the onion and celery and sauté until just soft.

Meanwhile, in a large bowl, soak the stuffing in the milk for about 5 minutes, until it is absorbed. Add the meat, onion, and celery, and stir to combine. Add the Maggi sauce, egg, tomato paste, salt, and pepper and mix thoroughly with your hands, making sure all the ingredients are well incorporated.

Line a Pyrex or similar glass baking dish with the bread slices. Place the meat mixture on the white bread and form into a loaf.

Bake for 1½ hours. Let rest 10 minutes before serving.

Slice the meat loaf and serve on a platter.

STUDENT'S RAGOUT

SERVES 6

When I was a child, my mom made this dish almost once a week in the autumn and winter months. She would make it in the electric frying pan, that long-forgotten kitchen gadget, and the whole house would smell delicious. This handy appliance is one of the few worth keeping in the cabinet for recipes just like this. Like many of my favorite dishes, this ragout is made in one pan, so cleanup is minimal. We preps without full-time help like that—a lot.

6 slices bacon
1½ pounds thin sliced beef top round, pounded cut into 8 pieces
1 teaspoon salt
1 teaspoon pepper
4 russet potatoes, peeled and thinly sliced

4 onions, thinly sliced
8 carrots, thinly sliced
½ cup water
1 loaf French bread
Pats of butter
¼ cup of ketchup

Place the bacon in a large deep sauté pan with a lid over medium-high heat or in an electric skillet with the temperature set to 375°F. Fry the bacon until slightly crisp, about 5 minutes, and then reduce the heat to low on the stovetop or to 300°F in an electric skillet.

Layer the beef pieces on top of the bacon, and sprinkle with a bit of the salt and pepper. Layer the potatoes on top of the beef, and sprinkle with the remaining salt and pepper. Layer the onions on top of the potatoes, and follow with the carrots. Pour the water over the top, and cover the pan.

Cook the ragout for 2 hours, checking the liquid level occasionally to make sure the bottom does not burn and adding more water as needed. Taste for seasoning, adding more salt and pepper as desired.

Serve with crusty bread, pats of butter, and a bowl of ketchup.

MAC AND CHEESE

SERVES 6

Just about everybody loves a good mac and cheese. It is by far one of our most requested catering dishes. The clients claim it is for the children, but then they order extra pans of it . . . just in case the adults want a little too.

There are a ton of variations on mac and cheese. Some are baked, some are made on the stovetop (like this one), and some are doctored up by a packet of bright orange powder. The trick to a really creamy mac and cheese is to use Velveeta or a good processed American cheese. I find that if you start with a sharp cheddar, the sauce has a bit of grit, which is not what anyone wants in a mac and cheese.

You can blend all sorts of things into mac and cheese, turning it into a one-pot supper. I, however, am a purist. I want my mac and cheese to stand alone. Well, a nice slice of meat loaf on the side wouldn't hurt!

4 tablespoons butter
½ cup flour
1½ cups whole milk
1 cup heavy cream
4 ounces cubed Velveeta or American cheese
2 ounces shredded sharp cheddar cheese

2 ounces shredded Havarti cheese
2 ounces crumbled blue cheese
1 teaspoon dry mustard
1 teaspoon salt
1 teaspoon white pepper
6 cups fully cooked elbow macaroni

In a large heavy-bottomed saucepan, melt the butter over medium heat. Sprinkle the flour into pan and stir, forming a roux. Cook over low heat for about 5 minutes to get the raw flour taste out of the mixture. Slowly whisk in the milk and cream, forming a béchamel sauce. Continue to stir, making sure not to burn the bottom of the pan, for 15 minutes.

Now, add the Velveeta cheese, whisking until it melts and thoroughly incorporates. Do the same with the cheddar, the Havarti, and the blue cheese. Whisk in the dry mustard. Taste and add salt and white pepper as needed.

Turn off the heat and slowly fold the macaroni into the sauce.

Serve immediately.

As a variation, transfer to a baking dish, top with crumbled potato chips and saltines, and bake at 350°F for 10 minutes.

Notes: If you don't like blue cheese, you can double the cheddar or the Havarti cheese. Don't cook the pasta to al dente. Cook it like you were going to just butter it and eat it as is.

CALF'S LIVER, BACON, AND ONIONS

SERVES 4

Liver is something that you either love or hate. If you have not tried it in a long time, I encourage you to try this liver recipe, which is from my aunt Joan. Most people have horrible childhood memories of liver that was overcooked to the point it resembled a chalky piece of shoe leather. Those memories alone can bring tears to the eyes.

Liver is actually quite tasty when cooked correctly, and it makes for a nice change of pace from the usual dinner. My aunt Joan chose not to cook, unless absolutely necessary. However, this is the one dish she would make. Make sure you purchase calf's liver and not beef liver. You do not want to eat beef liver, I assure you.

6 nice slices calf's liver (ask your butcher
   to slice them about ½ inch thick)
1 cup whole milk
8 slices bacon
2 tablespoons butter
3 large onions, thinly sliced

1½ teaspoons salt
1 teaspoon pepper
¾ cup flour
1 cup red wine
1½ cups beef stock or homemade veal
   stock (page 248)

Preheat the oven to 200°F.

In a nonreactive dish, soak the liver in the milk for 10 minutes or up to 12 hours in the refrigerator. In a large sauté pan, cook the bacon over medium heat until crisp, turning frequently, about 10 minutes. Remove the bacon from the pan, drain off the fat into a small bowl, and reserve.

In the same sauté pan, melt the butter over low heat, and cook the onions until nicely caramelized. Do not stir the onions until you see the onions at the bottom of the pan becoming golden brown. Now, stir frequently until they are all a beautiful golden brown. Be patient, caramelizing onions can take a while, up to 30 minutes. Season with ½ teaspoon of the salt and ½ teaspoon of the pepper. Remove the onions from the pan and reserve.

On a plate, stir together the flour with the remaining teaspoon salt and ½ teaspoon pepper. Working in batches, remove the liver from the milk and immediately dredge in the seasoned flour. Reserve 3 tablespoons of the remaining flour.

Return the bacon fat to the same sauté pan and raise the heat to medium-high. Working in batches, cook 2 or 3 liver slices over high heat, making sure not to crowd the pan or scorch the liver, for 1½ minutes. Flip the liver and cook 1½ minutes more. The liver will be slightly crispy on the outside, but pink in the center. Transfer the liver to a plate and keep warm in the oven until the remaining liver slices are cooked. Drain off all but 3 tablespoons of the fat.

Add the flour to the pan and stir until combined with the bacon fat. Add the red wine and whisk. A thick paste will form. Add the stock and continue to whisk vigorously until well incorporated. Continue to whisk the gravy, for an additional five minutes. Add the caramelized onions to the gravy and stir until well coated.

Remove the liver from the oven and add any drippings from the liver to the gravy.

Transfer the liver to six warmed plates, topping with the onions and gravy. Coarsely crumble the bacon over each liver slice and serve immediately.

THE COVERED DISH POTLUCK SUPPER

Preppies really don't do potlucks. If we cannot manage to provide a meal for our guests, we simply don't have a party. A progressive dinner, we don't mind (you know, the fun neighborhood party where appetizers are served at one house, entrees at another, and dessert at a final home). In this instance, we prefer to be a guest rather than a host and offer to stock the bar. And, of course, at a church fund-raising supper, we oblige, although we usually choose to make a side dish.

FROZEN GRASSHOPPER PIE

MAKES 1 PIE

Growing up, I always loved "icebox" desserts. Frozen, tasty, and usually containing whipped cream, ice cream, and chocolate or peanut butter, they are a cinch to whip up. Many believe this treat is based on the grasshopper cocktail. A classic dessert from the seventies, this pie combines the great flavor of mint and chocolate. Most important, it is a lovely pale green color thanks to a generous shot of crème de menthe and it looks great served on a pink plate. An added plus: It gives you a good reason to always keep marshmallows in your pantry.

FOR THE CRUST
20 chocolate cream cookies or Oreos
2 tablespoons melted butter

FOR THE FILLING
24 marshmallows

⅔ cup whole milk
3 tablespoons green crème de menthe
2 tablespoons clear crème de cacao
1 cup heavy cream
½ cup whipped cream or Cool Whip for garnish

For the crust: In a food processor, pulse the cookies until a fine crumb forms. Add the melted butter and pulse just until you can form a ball with the crumb and butter. Pour the crumb mixture into a 9-inch Pyrex pie plate and press evenly into the bottom and sides. Reserve any extra crumbs for garnish.

For the filling: In a medium saucepan, heat the marshmallows and milk over very low heat, about 7 minutes, or until melted. Set the pan aside to cool, stirring occasionally, about 20 minutes. When completely cooled, add the crème de menthe and crème de cacao. Whip the remaining cream until it's nearly stiff and firm peaks form. Fold into the cooled marshmallow mixture and pour into the prepared pie pan.

Sprinkle with a few crumbs from the crust mix.

Freeze overnight.

Slice and serve with a dollop of whipped cream or, if you're feeling really retro-campy, Cool Whip.

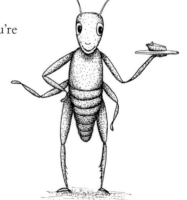

SUMMER

AND THE

LIVING IS EASY

SO IS THE EATING AND, OF COURSE, THE QUAFFING

Preppies love summer, but then again, doesn't everyone? Heading to the lake or beach house and opening it up for the season removes every care in the world. Or, at the very least, heading to your friend's summer house and being the guest who never leaves. Summer is delicious with its barbecues, long weekends, the big three picnic holidays—Memorial Day, Fourth of July, and then, sadly, Labor Day.

It's also a great time of year to grill more and turn on the oven less. If I'm cooking indoors in the summer I tend to do everything early in the morning, before the heat of the day. Besides, the allure of the outdoors does me in. The vegetables just scream to be plucked off the vine or handpicked from farmers' markets.

LOBSTER ROLLS

MAKES 4 LOBSTER ROLLS

Lobster rolls have become such a craze in the past few years. But the fact is this Down East treat has been around forever. I remember buying one at the McDonald's in Bar Harbor, Maine, back in the big eighties just to see what a fast-food lobster roll tasted like. And I have to admit, it wasn't half bad. Lobster rolls are decadent sandwiches and quite a treat to grab and go. It's the perfect bite of summer to take on a picnic, on a sail, or to the backyard to relish the flavor.

This recipe is for a traditional lobster roll. The fresh lobster meat and the split-top hot dog roll, well buttered, are the stars of the sandwich.

2 bay leaves
2 1¼-pound lobsters
½ cup good-quality mayonnaise
1 stalk celery, finely chopped

Juice of ½ lemon
2 tablespoons salted butter, softened
4 New England (called split-top) hot dog buns, such as Arnold's

Have a large bowl of ice water ready that is big enough to fit the lobsters next to the stove.

In a large stockpot with a lid, bring 8 quarts of water to a boil over high heat. Add the bay leaves and lobsters and let the water return to the boil. Cover, reduce to a simmer for 15 minutes. With tongs, transfer the lobsters to the bowl of ice water. Let cool.

Remove the lobster meat from the shells, making sure you get every bit. If you have never cracked a lobster, begin by twisting the tail from the body. Remove the tail, and check the bottom fin for any meat. Remove the large vein and any green (tamale) or bright red (roe) sacs. Twist the claws and knuckles, at the base of body and crack with a nut cracker. Use a skewer or any thin sharp object to get every bit of that knuckle meat out. The claws and knuckles have the sweetest, most tender meat.

Cut the meat into generous chunks, leaving the claws intact to top each roll with.

In a large bowl, toss the lobster meat with the mayonnaise and celery. Squeeze on the lemon juice and fold gently.

Generously spread butter on the top and outer sides of the rolls. Place the rolls in a sauté pan over medium heat until the butter has melted and all sides of the roll are golden brown.

Stuff each roll with the lobster mixture, garnish with a claw, and serve.

NEW POTATO SALAD WITH DILL

SERVES 6

There are about as many recipes for potato salad as there are potatoes in Idaho. This red-skinned version has very few ingredients, so once the potatoes are cooked, it can be mixed together in minutes and ready to serve as soon as it has cooled well. Toss the warm potatoes into the dressing so that they absorb the flavor.

4 cups new red-skinned potatoes, quartered
1 cup sour cream
½ cup mayonnaise

1 small red onion, finely diced
1 tablespoon cider vinegar
2 tablespoons fresh dill, finely chopped
Salt and pepper to taste

Put the potatoes in a large pot and add enough cold water to cover. Bring to a boil over high heat. Reduce the heat to medium and cook for about 25 minutes, or until the potatoes pierce easily with a fork. Drain.

In a large bowl, combine the sour cream, mayonnaise, onion, vinegar, and dill. Add the potatoes and toss until evenly coated. Taste and add salt and pepper as needed.

Chill for a few hours for the best flavor. Serve cold.

TOMATO PLATTER

Really, when summer tomatoes are flooding roadside stands, farmers' markets, and even the local grocery stores, there is not much need for anything else as a side dish to a meal. While most people like to serve them with basil, fresh mozzarella cheese, and a drizzle of balsamic vinegar, I like to keep it pristine.

I pick a bunch of pretty, colorful tomatoes, slice them up, layer them on a platter and sprinkle them with a hint of fleur de sel (fancy French sea salt that really is amazing). I don't think summer tomatoes need any other adornment or flavor.

THE PERFECT SUMMER SANDWICH

My dad always had a large vegetable garden. He would spend the winter days—when he couldn't play golf—going through seed catalogs and designing his garden layout for the next spring. Our next-door neighbor, Mae, gardened with him. It was a love affair over vegetables.

By early February, Dad had grow lights in the basement and seedlings starting to sprout. By April, the little plants were spending time outside in a cold frame for a few hours a day. In May, he would be vying for space in the garden with my mother and Mae's husband, Henry, who both wanted flowers everywhere. By July, the garden was in full swing with tomatoes, cucumbers, squash, and any other vegetable he could squeeze into the soil. Mommy's and Henry's flowers, by the way, had their space, too, and made everybody smile.

At lunchtime Dad would grab a tomato and cucumber, both still warm from the vine, and thinly slice them up. He'd layer them on white bread with just a little mayonnaise, salt, and pepper.

It was the best sandwich I've ever eaten. Give it a try.

Or for that perfect dripping-down-the-elbows summer-tomato sandwich, try these variations of a BLT:

- Bacon, avocado, tomato, and Havarti cheese on whole-grain bread

- Smoked salmon, tomato, and cucumber with a little sour cream on pumpernickel bread

- Bacon, lettuce, tomato, and blue cheese with honey mustard on white toast

- Bacon, lettuce, tomato, and Swiss cheese, with Thousand Island dressing on rye bread

BACON 101

When I am cooking bacon, I like to use my cast-iron skillet and cook it over a low flame, but baking it is much more efficient if you are cooking more than four or five slices. To do that, simply lay the bacon in a single layer on a jelly roll pan or baking sheet and bake at 375°F for 25 minutes. (If the bacon is really thinly sliced, check it at 10 minutes.)

EAST ENDER

This refreshing cocktail is comprised of a triple threat of prep. It is named after a section of London (Britain, preppy), made with gin (the prep alcohol of choice), and a hint of mint that is slightly reminiscent of a mint julep (Southern preppy). It is perfect for a late-summer afternoon cocktail, best served right after a brisk sail.

3 slices cucumber, plus one peel of
   cucumber for garnish
6 mint leaves
2 fluid ounces gin

1 ounce fresh lime juice
¾ ounce simple syrup
Ice cubes

Chill an old-fashioned glass.

In a cocktail shaker, lightly crush the cucumber slices and mint with a muddler. Add the gin, lime juice, simple syrup, and a handful of ice cubes. Shake well.

Strain into the chilled glass. Float shaved cucumber on top.

Repeat, and repeat, and repeat . . .

SUMMER SQUASH SALAD

SERVES 4 AS A FIRST COURSE

My restaurant Picnic opened in the month of July and the weather hit 101 degrees on the first day. I knew I needed plenty of salads on the menu, and I wanted a few that were not loaded with mixed greens. This simple summer squash salad did the trick. It screams summer, with the crisp texture of the squash and the lovely colors. Make sure to add the vinaigrette at the very last moment, as the squash will absorb it quickly.

Zest and juice of 2 lemons
⅓ cup vegetable or corn oil
2 tablespoons honey
1 teaspoon dry mustard
1 teaspoon salt
1 teaspoon black pepper

1 teaspoon red pepper flakes
8 small zucchini and yellow squash (about 2 pounds), unpeeled and rinsed well
⅓ cup pine nuts, toasted
2 ounces Parmesan cheese

In a large bowl or a blender, combine the lemon juice, zest, and oil. Whisk by hand or blend on low speed for 3 minutes, until emulsified. Add the honey, mustard, salt, and black pepper and whisk or blend on low speed until well incorporated. Taste for acidity and seasoning and add more salt and pepper as needed. Stir in the lemon zest and the pepper flakes.

Using a mandoline or a vegetable peeler, slice thin ribbons of squash into a large bowl. Once there are lots of seeds in the squash and little flesh, stop and move on to the next squash. Add the dressing and the pine nuts and toss until evenly coated.

Divide evenly among the chilled plates and, with a vegetable peeler, shave the cheese over the squash. Serve.

CHICKEN WITH BLUEBERRY BARBECUE SAUCE

SERVES 4

Grilled skin-on chicken is delicious but also a bit tricky to pull off. That pesky skin just sticks to the grates. My trick is to cook the chicken skin side up, over medium heat, and with the grill cover closed, which crisps the skin. I add the barbecue sauce during the final minute or two of cooking, so that it doesn't burn. I adore the flavors of fruit with savory dishes and this sauce is loaded with the taste of summer blueberries. Additionally, the barbecue sauce has a blue tint to it, making it a colorful addition to a patriotic cookout.

2 2½-pound fryer chickens, cut into thighs, drumsticks, breasts, and wings (or any way you choose)
2 teaspoons kosher salt

2 teaspoons coarsely ground pepper
2 tablespoon butter, melted
1½ cups Blueberry Barbecue Sauce (recipe follows)

Preheat a gas grill to medium, set up for indirect cooking heat or prepare a charcoal grill for indirect grilling (see page 54).

Season the chicken with the salt and pepper. Place the chicken pieces, skin side up, on the grill. Cover and grill, checking every 10 minutes to make sure the chicken is not sticking to the grill and rotating the chicken pieces to ensure even cooking. Do not flip the chicken or the skin will stick to the grill. Brush the chicken occasionally with the butter. Cook until the chicken registers 160°F on an instant-read thermometer, about 20 to 25 minutes. The wings will cook fastest, the breasts longer. As they are done, transfer the chicken pieces to a platter.

When all the chicken is cooked, return it to the grill and brush the skin lightly with the barbecue sauce, reserving the remaining sauce for serving. Cook 2 minutes more. Serve with the remaining barbecue sauce.

BLUEBERRY BARBECUE SAUCE

MAKES ABOUT 1½ PINTS

3 garlic cloves, crushed
¼ cup minced onion
2 tablespoons olive oil
2 cups ketchup
¼ cup water
3 tablespoons cider vinegar
2 tablespoons tomato paste
1 tablespoon Worcestershire sauce
1 tablespoon soy sauce

⅓ cup packed light brown sugar
2 tablespoons chili powder
1 tablespoon ground cumin
1 tablespoon coarsely ground black
  pepper
1 teaspoon dry mustard
½ teaspoon cayenne pepper
3 cups fresh blueberries
juice of ½ lemon

In a heavy-bottomed saucepan over medium heat, sweat the garlic and onion in the oil for about 5 minutes. Add the ketchup, water, vinegar, tomato paste, Worcestershire sauce, and soy sauce and stir until combined. Add the brown sugar, chili powder, cumin, black pepper, dry mustard, and cayenne and stir until combined. Cook for 30 minutes, stirring frequently. Add the blueberries and cook for 45 minutes more, stirring frequently, until the blueberries have completely broken down and the sauce is somewhat chunky. Stir in the lemon juice.

Let cool or serve warm.

Refrigerate for up to 1 week in a sealed container.

"CHEATERS" SLOW-BARBECUED PORK BELLY

SERVES A CROWD

In late summer, when things start to cool off a bit, I love making a whole pork belly. For the uninitiated, the pork belly is just that—the belly of the pork, fatty, crisp-skinned, and delicious. It is also the cut of pork used for bacon. The longer you let it cook, the more the fat will melt into the meat, creating a lush, succulent dish that's perfect to serve with a light salad and baked beans (see page 61).

The cheating part of this dish is that, before grilling, I cook it in a 225°F oven for about four hours. It's perfect to cook with the baked beans, which cook at that same temperature. By the time the pork belly hits the grill, a lot of the fat has melted, which stops crazy flare-ups from the hot coals.

1 large boneless pork belly (about 12 pounds), skin removed by your butcher
1 cup chicken stock
2 stalks celery
2 large sweet onions, thickly sliced
½ cup packed light brown sugar
¼ cup kosher salt

¼ cup ground cumin
3 tablespoons ground cinnamon
3 tablespoons coarsely ground pepper
2 tablespoons ground allspice
2 tablespoons ground nutmeg
2 tablespoons paprika

Preheat the oven to 225°F.

In a large roasting pan, place the pork belly, fatty side up. Cut the pork belly into two portions to fit, if needed. Add the stock, celery, and onions.

In a medium bowl, add the brown sugar, salt, cumin, cinnamon, pepper, allspice, nutmeg, and paprika and mix well. Slather generously all over the top of the pork.

Cover the pork with parchment paper, then tightly cover the roasting pan with foil.

Put the pork in the oven. Find something else to do for about 2 hours (maybe make those beans I suggest to go with it?), then check the pork to ensure that there is still a bit of liquid in the base of the roasting pan. Add water if needed. Continue cooking for 2 hours more.

Remove the pork from the oven. After 4 hours of cooking, the pork should be wildly tender, and a lot of the fat should have melted to the bottom of the pan. Let the pork rest, in the pan, for about 45 minutes. Discard the celery and onions.

While the pork rests, prepare the grill. If using charcoal, set the coals for indirect cooking (see page 54) When the coals have died down to low, place the pork as far away from the coals as possible.

If using a gas grill, light only the back burner on low.

Cover and grill for 1 hour, or until the pork fat is crispy and golden brown.

Transfer the pork to a platter and cover loosely with foil. Let rest for about 20 minutes.

Carve, against the grain, into thick slices. Arrange on a large platter and serve.

HINTS FOR THE GRILL

You don't need to be a pit master to really use the grill to your advantage. And while summer is the ultimate grilling time, I fire up the gas grill all year round, despite the chilly East Coast winters. However, given my druthers, I prefer a charcoal grill fortified with some fallen branches from the yard.

Grilling with hardwoods imparts a unique flavor to the food, especially when cooking over low heat; and it smells great, too. Of course, you'll also get that preppy satisfaction of recycling your yard waste and being oh so outdoorsy at the same time.

INDIRECT GRILLING

I like cooking over indirect heat, which simply means you fill half the kettle with the coals (I prefer hardwood coals to charcoal briquettes) and wood, and use the half of the grill without the coals for cooking. You need to keep the lid on the kettle to allow the hot air to circulate and slowly cook, almost roast, your food. Lift the lid every once in a while to check for doneness and to get some air into the coals so they do not extinguish. That's how you can get fall-off-the-bone ribs, moist roasted chicken without a burned skin, and a smoky flavor to your pork belly (see page 52). If using a gas grill, only light the back burner and try to keep your food as far to the front of the grill as possible. Always keep the lid on, checking frequently for any burning.

DIRECT GRILLING

To set up a charcoal grill for direct grilling add the coals to the center of the grill, making a nice large pile. Light, and when the fire has died down and the coals are a glowing red, spread them evenly over the grill. Leave a quarter of the grill without coals, for keeping finished food warm. Cook directly on the hot grill, uncovered.

For a gas grill, light all the burners to high and cover. When the temperature of the grill hits 500°F, turn the burners to medium high and cook your food uncovered.

LOBSTER BAKE FOR A CROWD

SERVES 20-30 HEALTHY EATERS

The reality is that not all of us (myself included) are lucky enough to have beach-front property, which would allow us to dig a big hole in the sand, light some coals, and get a lobster bake going. But with the apparatus and method I describe here, you can have a lobster bake anywhere, even in a parking lot. A bake is great for a big tailgate party.

This takes an afternoon so the time is perhaps best spent with a cold beer or gin and tonic.

SPECIAL EQUIPMENT
1 30-gallon galvanized garbage can and lid with 15 3-inch square airholes cut into it (5 near the bottom, 5 in the center, and 5 near the top)
10 pounds Charcoal and/or hardwood
Burlap bag
10 pounds rock or gravel stone
Bag of seaweed (ask your fishmonger)

1 bushel littleneck or cherrystone clams, scrubbed
1 bushel mussels, such as Prince Edward Island, scrubbed and debearded

10 pounds sausage of your choice, such as sweet Italian
10 pounds new potatoes or Yukon Gold potatoes
3 pounds sweet onions, peeled
2 dozen ears corn, husks and silks removed
20 1- to 1¼-pound lobsters (Pick them up the day of the lobster bake—preferably while someone else is setting up the bake—and have your fish monger kill them immediately for you. Keep ice cold until ready to cook.)
2 pounds salted butter, melted

In the base of the garbage can, light the charcoal and hardwood and let heat for two hours, until the flames have died down and the coals are piping hot and bright red.

Have a damp burlap cloth ready. Add rocks on top of the coals.

Working quickly, add a layer of seaweed, followed by the clams and mussels, and then the sausages. Add a layer of potatoes and onions, followed by the corn.

Add the lobsters on top of the corn

Cover with the damp burlap cloth and place the lid on the can. Let steam 1 hour, or until the clams and mussels have opened and the lobsters are a nice bright red.

Serve with lots of melted butter and plenty of napkins.

OYSTERS AND CLAMS
ON THE GRILL
SERVES 4

One of the best meals I've ever eaten was at a friend's house out on the North Fork of Long Island, the more bucolic prong of the East End. The area has an easygoing vibe and is dotted with wineries, farmstands, and fish markets. The meal we prepared was simple and included some oysters and clams from the Peconic Bay that we literally had watched the fishermen unload. We also picked up local tomatoes and corn from an honor system farmstand. Our final stop was at one of the terrific wineries for a bottle of chardonnay. We picked fresh herbs from the garden and created the epitome of a local, seasonal meal with fresh sautéed corn and a platter of tomatoes. I can still taste it.

5 tablespoons salted butter
½ medium shallot, minced
1 cup chicken stock
½ cup dry white wine
1 tablespoon fresh tarragon leaves
1 tablespoon torn fresh basil leaves

1 tablespoon fresh thyme leaves
2 teaspoons pepper
3 dozen oysters (Blue Points are just swell, but any will do in a pinch)
3 dozen littleneck clams, scrubbed

Set up the grill for direct cooking (see page 54).

While the grill heats up, make the sauce. In a large sauté pan, melt the butter over medium heat. Slowly sweat the shallot for about 3 minutes. Add the stock and wine, and simmer for 5 minutes. Stir in the tarragon, basil, thyme, and pepper. Reduce the heat to low, and keep warm until ready to serve.

Place the oysters on the grill directly over the heat. Close the lid and grill for 5 minutes. Add the clams alongside the oysters and grill for 5 to 10 minutes more, or until their shells open. Keep the lid on the grill, but open it and check it every couple of minutes. As soon as the shells open, transfer them to a large bowl or platter.

Pour the sauce over the warm oysters and clams.

SAUTÉED FRESH CORN

SERVES 4

Corn may very well be *the* summer vegetable. Tales are often told of a pot of boiling water waiting for corn being picked right at that moment. I've been lucky enough to taste that just-picked flavor and it is memorable beyond belief. When I was maybe ten years old, I spent a few weeks in Maine, where my uncle Witt had a gorgeous garden. My cousin Gwen and I went out to pick corn with him while my aunt put the water on to boil. We shucked the ears as we ran toward the house, and threw them gleefully into the pot.

Now, here's the thing, my aunt didn't let that corn sit in the water for more than a minute and a half. The second the water came back to a boil, she pulled them out. Slathered in butter, it was such a wonderful treat. The reality is, most people overcook corn. Another reality is that eating corn on the cob is not the most attractive activity. Butter dripping down your chin is fine, as long as you are not entertaining. My mom always insisted we "score our corn" with a little corn scorer she set at each place at the table so the corn would not squirt in the face of the diner sitting opposite.

This corn dish is easy to prepare and polite to eat; the timing is very important. One more thing: Buy the freshest corn possible, and if you are not cooking it immediately, pop it into the fridge until you're ready to cook. The cold of the fridge will slow down the process of the sugars turning to starch.

8 ears fresh corn, husks and silks removed
3 tablespoons butter

1 tablespoon fresh thyme leaves
½ teaspoon salt
½ teaspoon pepper

Remove the kernels from the ears of corn. To do this, lay a small tea towel in a bowl and place the bottom of the ear in the center of the bowl. Hold the very top of the corn, and using a chef's knife, cut the corn from the cob in rows.

In a large sauté pan, melt the butter over medium heat. Crank the heat to high and add the corn, thyme, salt, and pepper, shaking the sauté pan constantly and stirring slowly. Cook for 1½ minutes, and transfer to a serving bowl. Serve immediately.

WALNUT-CRUSTED HALIBUT FILLETS WITH MIXED BERRY AND THYME GASTRIQUE

SERVES 4

Halibut is a wonderful, flaky white fish, albeit one of the most expensive. It has a very low fat content, making it fall apart and dry out easily if overcooked. The mixed berry and thyme sauce lends a nice counterbalance of sweet and savory.

2 tablespoons butter
1 shallot, minced
½ cup fresh blueberries
½ cup fresh blackberries
3 tablespoons sugar
1 tablespoon water
3 tablespoons white wine vinegar
Juice of 1½ lemons
1 tablespoon fresh thyme leaves or
    1 teaspoon dried

1 teaspoon kosher salt
1 teaspoon freshly cracked pepper
½ cup panko bread crumbs
½ cup toasted walnut pieces
4 6-ounce portions of halibut
⅓ cup dry white wine
Juice of 1 lemon
1 tablespoon butter, cut in small cubes
3 tablespoons Dijon mustard
3 tablespoons mayonnaise

Preheat the oven to 375°F.

First, make the gastrique. In a saucepan, melt 1 tablespoon of the butter over medium heat. Add the shallot and cook until just translucent, about 3 minutes. Add the blueberries and blackberries, and cover with the sugar. Cook over low heat, stirring frequently, for about 5 minutes. Add the water, vinegar, and juice from half a lemon and raise the heat to high. Bring to a boil, then reduce the heat to medium low. Add the thyme, salt, and pepper and simmer for about 30 minutes, until the berries start to break down. Reduce the heat to low and keep warm until ready to serve with the fish.

In a food processor, combine the panko and the walnuts, pulsing until the walnuts are finely chopped.

Place the halibut fillets, presentation side up, in a nonreactive baking dish. Pour the wine and remaining lemon juice around the fillets doing the same with pats of the remaining tablespoon butter.

In a small bowl, combine the Dijon and the mayonnaise and slather the top of each fillet with a ¼ inch of the mixture. Press the panko-walnut mixture onto the Dijon-mayonnaise mixture firmly to adhere.

Bake for 10 minutes, depending on the thickness, or until the halibut begins to lightly flake with a fork.

Transfer to warmed plates and spoon the gastrique over each fillet. Serve immediately.

PEG DAY'S BAKED BEANS

SERVES 8-10

These beans have been served at my family's cookouts for decades. As a matter of fact, my aunt Peggy, whose recipe it was, would always serve them at her Christmas Day buffet. They are just about the best baked beans I've ever had. If you have a bean pot (a deep ceramic pot with handles and a tight-fitting lid), it's best to cook them in that. If not, a casserole will do in a pinch. I've left much of the verbiage from Aunt Peggy's original recipe, since, well, there is no other way to explain some things.

1 pound dried navy beans or great
    northern beans, picked through,
    rinsed, and soaked overnight in the
    refrigerator
½ teaspoon baking soda

½ pound salt pork
½ teaspoon dry mustard
½ teaspoon pepper
3 tablespoons sugar
1 cup water

Preheat the oven to 225°F.

Drain the beans, and put in a large pot. Add enough water to cover and add the baking soda. Slowly bring to a boil over medium heat. Cook until the skin blows off the beans, about 20 minutes. Drain and return to the bean pot. Add the salt pork.

In a small saucepan, mix the mustard, pepper, and sugar with the water. Bring to a boil over medium high heat and pour over the beans. Add more water as needed so that the beans are fully covered with liquid.

Transfer the pot to the oven and bake, covered, for 7 hours, checking occasionally that there is a bit of liquid remaining. Uncover the pot and cook 1 hour more. Serve directly from the bean pot.

GIN AND TONIC

o introduction needed. It is The Drink.

4 large ice cubes
3 fluid ounces best-quality gin, such as
   Bombay Sapphire

3 fluid ounces tonic water
1 tablespoon lime juice
Lime wedge, for garnish

Fill a highball glass with the ice cubes. Add the gin, tonic, and lime juice. Stir. Garnish with the lime wedge.

GRILLED CHEESE CASSEROLE

SERVES 4

When our garden was overflowing with tomatoes my mother made them the star of a casserole that was very reminiscent of a grilled cheese sandwich. Kids would eat them that way. While I am sure most shredded cheeses would work fine, there is something about using American cheese that is just right for the dish. It goes great with any grilled meats, and is quick to assemble.

8 slices American cheese, cut into 2-inch strips

4 or 5 ripe tomatoes, such as Jersey beefsteak, cut into 2-inch wedges, no need to be accurate

10 slices pullman or other white bread, cut into 2-inch cubes

3 tablespoons butter, cut into small cubes

1 teaspoon salt

1 teaspoon pepper

Preheat the oven to 350°F. Generously butter a 9 x 13-inch Pyrex or similar glass baking dish.

In a large bowl, combine the cheese, tomatoes, and bread. Lightly press the bread mixture into the casserole, and dot the top with the butter cubes.

Bake for 15 minutes, or until the cheese is melted and starting to turn golden brown. Let rest 5 minutes before serving.

PORK with PEACHES and MUSTARD

SERVES 4

Ipersonally love breaded fried pork. The crisp breading harks back to the days of Shake 'N Bake and jarred applesauce. These lightly fried cutlets pair just right with the sweet and zesty peach compote. Pork cooks quickly, so it's perfect for a mid-week dinner. I buy the thin-cut boneless loin pork chops and pound them even thinner. Of course, you can also buy a small pork roast and slice it yourself.

FOR THE PORK
½ cup flour
1 tablespoon salt
1 tablespoon pepper
4 eggs
2 cups panko bread crumbs
4 boneless thin-cut loin pork chops, pounded to ¼ inch thickness
2 cups vegetable oil

FOR THE COMPOTE
2 ripe peaches or any stone fruit, such as apricot, nectarine, or plums, cut into 1-inch cubes
1½ tablespoons Pommery mustard
½ teaspoon salt
2 tablespoons chopped fresh flat-leaf parsley

Preheat the oven to 175°F.

For the pork: On a plate, stir together the flour, salt, and pepper. Beat the eggs in a shallow dish. Spread the panko on a second plate.

Working with 1 pork chop at a time, dredge in the seasoned flour, dip in egg, then coat in the panko, pressing firmly to adhere. Repeat until all pork chops are breaded.

In a large sauté pan, heat the oil over high heat until it reaches 375°F. Carefully lower 2 cutlets into the oil and fry for 2 minutes, until just golden brown. Flip and fry for 2 minutes more, until the other side is golden. Remove the pork from the oil and transfer to a baking rack in the oven to keep warm until the remaining pork chops are cooked.

For the compote: In a large bowl, mix the peaches, mustard, salt, and parsley.

To serve: Top each cutlet with compote. Serve immediately.

NO WORRIES ABOUT A RAINOUT!

The menu is planned, as unassuming as can be. A lovely rib-eye steak, simply sliced fresh tomatoes with a hint of salt, and a crisp green salad. You are about to light the grill when you notice the wind kick up, and the gray clouds looming overhead. A downpour is imminent. You have two choices: grab a slicker from the mudroom or, better yet, a cast-iron skillet and a bottle of Maggi sauce.

What is Maggi sauce, you ask? It is a salty (very salty) condiment from Switzerland that made its way to the States; it's almost like soy sauce sans the soy. If you've ever had a sizzling steak at a restaurant, chances are Maggi is what made it taste so salty and yummy.

So simply take out that trusty cast-iron skillet and get it nice and hot over high heat. Let it heat up for a good three minutes. Throw 2 teaspoons of butter in and add about six dashes of Maggi. Immediately put the steak into the sizzling butter and cook for about 1½ minutes on each side (assuming it's ½-inch- to ¾-inch-thick rib-eye), until medium-rare. Immediately transfer the steak to a plate, pour the butter sauce over it, and let rest for a few minutes. Keep making the steaks until all have been fried up. Place them on platters, but do not stack the steaks; the heat will make them keep cooking.

PEACH CRISP

SERVES 8-10

Everyone has a different way to make a fruit crisp; some like brown sugar, nuts, or even granola in the topping. This is a less embellished version of a crisp and calls for fresh peaches, which I use when they are in season. As soon as autumn comes along, I switch to apples.

8 to 10 peaches, peeled and thickly sliced
1 tablespoon lemon juice
1 cup plus 1 tablespoon sugar

¾ cups flour
½ cup butter, cubed, plus 1 tablespoon butter for greasing the dish

Preheat the oven to 350°F.

Lightly butter a 9 x 13-inch Pyrex or similar baking dish. Add the peaches and lemon juice and stir. Sprinkle with 1 tablespoon of the sugar.

In a food processor, combine the flour, the remaining 1 cup of sugar, and the butter, and pulse until small crumbs form. Press the flour mixture firmly over the peaches to adhere, making sure to cover the entire surface.

Bake for 40 minutes, or until the crisp is light golden brown.

Serve warm or at room temperature.

ROASTED STONE FRUITS
WITH HONEY AND WALNUTS

SERVES 4

hen summer has come to its bitter end and the nights begin to cool, a warm bowl of roasted stone fruit topped with a bit of ice cream celebrates the last flavors of the season.

8 assorted stone fruits, such as peaches, nectarines, plums, and apricots, halved
4 tablespoons butter, cut into 1-inch cubes

⅓ cup honey
1 cup dry-roasted walnuts
1 tablespoon fresh cracked pepper

Preheat oven to 400°F. Lightly grease a 9 x 13-inch baking dish.

Arrange the stone fruits, skin side down, in the dish and top with the butter. Roast for 20 minutes. Remove dish from the oven and stir. Add the honey and stir again. Roast for 5 minutes more, until the fruits are softened and beginning to turn golden.

Stir in the walnuts and the pepper. Serve immediately.

THE

SPORTING

LIFE

Preps play golf, but anxiously await the nineteenth hole. We sail, but always pack a lunch and a cocktail. We play tennis, but after we sweat, we are more interested in the gin and tonic than the score. And we certainly love a good spectator event. Why? It's simply one more excuse for a great party! From breakfast at Wimbledon to the Kentucky Derby (if possible, you attend in person instead of watching it on television) to a great football tailgate (professional or college, preferably your alma mater) we are there, with sandwiches, drinks, and a smile.

WILLOW HILL
FARM
HORSE
SHOW

SUSSEX
COUNTY
HORSE
SHOW

TRI
COUNTY
HORSE
SHOW
SERIES

SUSSEX
COUNTY

WILLOW HILL
FARM
HORSE
SHOW

HORSE
SHOW
SERIES

RESERVE
CHAMPION

Champion

Champion

WILLOW HILL
FARM
HORSE
SHOW

RESERVE
CHAMPION

1995

2008

SUSSEX
COUNTY

SUSSEX
COUNTY
HORSE

WARM MARINATED OLIVES

MAKES ABOUT 2 POUNDS

Believe it or not, there are other ways to marinate olives than just dropping them in a martini or two (and then getting marinated yourself). These olives are easy to whip up, nice to keep on hand, and when a last-minute occasion for a cocktail and snack arrives, they can be warmed up in two minutes flat.

2 pounds mixed olives of your choice
   (many olive bars sell a mixed blend)
¼ cup good-quality olive oil
Juice from ½ lemon, rind reserved and cut
   into ¼-inch strips

1 large sprig fresh rosemary
½ teaspoon fresh thyme leaves (lemon
   thyme if you have it)
1 tablespoon coarse black pepper

In a small bowl, mix the olives, oil, lemon juice and rind strips, rosemary, thyme, and pepper. Cover tightly with plastic wrap and let marinate in the fridge for up to 1 week.

To serve, put as many olives as the moment warrants in a small saucepan. Heat over low heat for about 2 minutes, until the olives are warm. Do not let the oil bubble. Serve immediately.

SPICY PECANS

Every year my mom's friend would give her a bag of pecans from the Smith College Club. Yes, the Smith College Club's fund-raiser has always been selling pecans. Often included with the one-pound bag were a few recipe cards, including one for this tasty snack. I started making these many years ago, and they are a nifty hostess gift.

2 tablespoons butter	½ teaspoon celery salt
1 tablespoon Worcestershire sauce	¼ teaspoon ground cumin
½ teaspoon garlic powder	⅛ teaspoon cayenne pepper
½ teaspoon seasoned salt	1½ cups raw pecan halves

Preheat the oven to 325°F.

In a medium sauté pan, melt the butter over low heat. Stir in the Worcestershire sauce until combined. Add the garlic powder, seasoned salt, celery salt, cumin, and cayenne, and simmer for 2 minutes, stirring constantly with a rubber spatula, until the spices start to give off a lovely scent. Turn off the heat. Fold in the pecans.

Spread the pecan mixture in a single layer on a baking sheet. Bake for 15 to 20 minutes, stirring occasionally and checking frequently to avoid burning.

Let cool. Store for up to one week in an airtight container.

PIMM'S CUP

nnabel, my friend and business partner when we ran the restaurant Picnic, hails from Wimbledon and has made this cocktail at the actual tennis event. This, in her British opinion, is the true recipe for this highly quaffable beverage.

2 tablespoons lemon juice
1 ½-inch slice peeled English cucumber
  (reserve the peel)
4 or 5 ice cubes

3 fluid ounces Pimm's No. 1
4 fluid ounces ginger ale or 7 Up
1 cucumber peel

In a highball glass, add the lemon juice and the slice of cucumber. Muddle slightly. Add 4 or 5 large ice cubes, Pimm's, and ginger ale. Stir. Garnish with the cucumber peel. Consume as if you were on the green grass of Wimbledon.

ORIGINAL CHEX MIX

For generations, Chex Mix has graced many a party with its presence. I found an old magazine ad with an original recipe from the Ralston Purina Company. I've changed it just a bit, replacing margarine with butter and omitting the Wheat Chex, since I am not a fan. Feel free to use either.

4 tablespoons butter
1¼ teaspoons seasoned salt
4½ tablespoons Worcestershire sauce
4 cups Corn Chex

4 cups Rice Chex
1 cup salted mixed nuts
1 cup mini pretzels

Preheat the oven to 250°F.

Melt the butter over medium-high heat in a roasting pan. Remove from heat and stir in the seasoned salt and the Worcestershire sauce. Gradually add the cereal, nuts, and pretzels, mixing until evenly coated.

Bake about 1 hour, stirring every 15 minutes. Transfer to a paper towel–lined baking sheet to cool. Store the mix in an airtight container for up to 5 days.

BRIDGE, THE SPORT OF LEISURE

During the day, when ladies had a bit more time on their hands, they would spend an afternoon, usually twice a month, playing their own special sport: bridge. Tea would be served first, and then the ladies would move to the bridge tables. The tables were covered with neat linen tablecloths, often in garish prints. Snacks included bridge mix (an assortment of chocolate-covered raisins, nuts, malted milk balls, and toffees) or chocolates. The playing cards were made by Caspari and had unique and pretty backs. Tallies to keep score matched perfectly.

The kid gloves were off, as bridge is a serious game that can take hours. There was no drinking during the event, except of more tea. The winning team would, however, rejoice at cocktail hour.

CHEESE TWISTS WITH OLIVES

MAKES 22 TWISTS

These spiffy twists are great to put on a cheese board, or serve with the Warm Marinated Olives (page 74) with cocktails before a casual dinner. The olives and anchovies are a nice addition to the usual cheese twists. If you hate anchovies, skip them. If you are not serving the twists immediately, cook them about two minutes less, then reheat them for about five minutes, right before serving.

Flour for the work surface
1 17.3-ounce package (2 sheets) puff pastry
1 egg beaten with 1 tablespoon water

½ cup pitted kalamata olives, finely chopped
2 anchovies, minced
½ cup shredded Parmesan cheese

Preheat the oven to 375°F. Line a baking sheet with a Silpat or buttered parchment paper.

On a lightly floured work surface, lightly roll out the puff pastry until it is 10 x 12 inches. Lightly brush with the egg wash.

With your hands, randomly scatter the olives and anchovies onto the pastry. Sprinkle the cheese evenly on top. Lightly press the pastry down with the palms of your hands. With a knife or pizza wheel, cut the sheet into twelve 10-inch-long strips.

Transfer the pastry strips to the prepared baking sheet. Carefully twist each strip until it resembles rope.

Bake for 10 to 12 minutes, until puffed and golden brown. Transfer to a wire rack to cool. Serve slightly warm.

Note: Silpats are nonstick silicone mats that let sticky foods, for instance cheese, slide right off the pan.

GRILLED PEAR, ROAST BEEF, AND BLUE CHEESE SANDWICHES

MAKES 2 SANDWICHES

ith its unique texture from the pear, coupled with the blue cheese, this sandwich offers a hint of autumn and is a nice nibble while watching the game.

4 slices hearty white bread, such as sourdough
6 thin slices rare roast beef
1 ripe pear, cored and thinly sliced

3 tablespoons crumbled blue cheese
1 tablespoon mayonnaise
1 tablespoon butter, softened

On two bread slices, layer the roast beef and the pear slices.

In a small bowl, mash the blue cheese and the mayonnaise with a fork. Spread the blue cheese mixture onto the remaining 2 bread slices, and place, blue cheese side down, onto the roast beef and pear slices.

Spread the outside of each sandwich with the butter. Place in a cold sauté pan on the stovetop over medium heat and cook for about 3 minutes, until golden brown. Flip the sandwiches and cook about 3 minutes more, until the other side is golden brown.

Cut the sandwiches in half and serve.

OBSCENE CHEESESTEAK SANDWICHES

MAKES 12 SANDWICHES

When I had just started my cooking career, I had a very small location called Picnic where I did catering and sold take-out lunches. Lunch was always a bit quiet, though we had our regulars. One day, in walked a writer from *The New York Times*, who wrote a small blurb that included a mention of this sandwich. From then on, our lunch business took off. I had to hire three more people just to be able to answer phones and do deliveries.

There is one caveat I should make about this sandwich. I hate, truly hate, any bell peppers, and there are few recipes in this book that include them. The fact is, when I make any of these dishes for myself, I leave out the peppers completely. I know most people don't have a pepper aversion, so I suffer through cooking them for their sakes.

1 5-pound beef tenderloin trimmed by butcher
1 pound butter, softened
3 teaspoons salt
5 large sweet onions, thinly sliced
6 garlic cloves, minced

3 orange bell peppers, cut into thin strips
3 yellow bell peppers, cut into thin strips
2 teaspoons black pepper
12 slices cheddar cheese
4 fresh sourdough baguettes

Preheat the oven to 400°F.

Place the beef on a baking sheet and rub with ¼ cup (1 stick) of the butter and 1 teaspoon of the salt. Roast the beef for 20 minutes; it will be very rare. Set aside to rest.

While the beef roasts, in a medium sauté pan, melt 4 tablespoons of the butter over low heat. Add the onions and garlic and reduce to very low heat, until the onions soften and caramelize. This is a labor of love and can take quite awhile, up to 30 minutes.

In another sauté pan, melt 2 tablespoons butter over low. Add the orange and yellow bell peppers and sauté for 10 minutes, until soft. Season with a pinch of salt and black pepper.

In a small saucepan, melt the remaining butter over low heat. While it melts, thinly slice the beef. Working in batches, place the beef slices into the butter until they reach medium-rare, or to your preferred level of doneness.

Slice the baguettes lengthwise and layer the bottom halves with the cheese, beef slices, onions, and peppers. Close the baguettes and press lightly. Cut into the portion sizes of your choice. Serve immediately.

BREAD AND BUTTER PICKLES

MAKES FOUR 1-QUART JARS

There is not much that beats a nice pickle—on a burger or next to a sandwich. This recipe has been in the family for a long time, and the pickles are just as they should be. If you don't want to can them, cut the recipe by three quarters and store the pickles for up to two weeks in the fridge.

4 quarts cucumbers, cut into ⅛-inch-thick
    slices
1 green bell pepper, cut into thin strips
6 onions, thinly sliced
⅓ cup salt

5 cups sugar
3 cups cider vinegar
2 tablespoons mustard seeds
1½ teaspoons turmeric
1½ teaspoons celery seeds

In a large bowl, cover the cucumbers, bell pepper, and onions with the salt. Cover with cracked ice cubes and let stand for three hours. Drain.

In a large stockpot, combine the cucumber mixture with the sugar, vinegar, mustard seeds, turmeric, and celery seeds.

Bring to a boil over high heat. Reduce the heat to medium high and simmer for 10 minutes, then immediately remove from heat.

To can the pickles: Prepare the canner, the jars, and the lids according to the manufacturer's instructions. Pack the pickles into hot jars and ladle the hot pickling juices over the cucumber slices leaving ½ inch head space. Remove any air bubbles, and wipe the rims of the jars. Center the lids on the jars and seal to just tight.

Process in a boiling water canner for 15 minutes. Pickles will keep up to 1 year.

BLUE RIBBON CHILI

SERVES 8

My mom always served chili over lettuce with saltine crackers on the side. I am not sure why, perhaps she wanted to add a vegetable to the meal. I like to serve it with saltines, but also a little sour cream and cheddar, the standard garnishes.

1½ pounds ground chuck (20% fat)
1 medium onion, chopped
1 carrot, thinly sliced
1¾ cups tomato puree
3 tablespoons tomato paste
1 15-ounce can kidney beans, rinsed
1 15-ounce can cannellini beans, rinsed
1 16-ounce can baked beans, such as
   Bush's
2 tablespoons chili powder, or to taste

1 teaspoon coarsely ground black pepper
1 teaspoon seasoned salt
½ teaspoon ground allspice
½ teaspoon ground cinnamon
Dash of ground chipotle pepper
Dash of cayenne pepper
½ cup shredded cheddar cheese
½ cup sour cream
1 sleeve saltine crackers

In a heavy-bottomed pot, cook the beef over medium heat for 15 minutes, or until brown. Add the onion and carrot and cook for 2 minutes. Drain off any excess fat. Add the tomato puree and tomato paste, and stir to combine. Add the kidney, cannellini, and baked beans, and stir to combine. Add the chili powder, black pepper, seasoned salt, allspice, cinnamon, chipotle pepper, and cayenne. Reduce the heat to low and slowly simmer for 2 hours, stirring frequently.

To serve, transfer the chili to a large bowl and serve with small bowls of cheddar and sour cream. Serve the saltines in their sleeve.

"ITALIAN" SANDWICHES

SERVES 4

Portland, Maine, is the home, so history tells us, of the Italian. Note that it is never called an Italian sandwich, just an "Italian." It is always on a very soft hoagie roll, and calls for American as its cheese. Very Italian, that! Perhaps someone thought the bell pepper made it Italian?

A true Maine Italian is a thing of beauty.

2 large soft hoagie rolls
8 slices American cheese
1 pound sliced deli ham
2 sour dill pickles, thinly sliced
1 tomato, thinly sliced
12 black olives, pitted

1 small onion, sliced
1 small green bell pepper, sliced
3 tablespoons olive oil
3 tablespoons red wine vinegar
Salt and pepper to taste

Cut the hoagie rolls lengthwise leaving about a ½ inch uncut. Layer the bottom halves of the rolls with cheese and ham followed by the pickles, tomato, olives, onion, and green pepper.

Drizzle each sandwich with the oil and vinegar and sprinkle with salt and pepper. Cut each sandwich in half and serve immediately.

HARVARD BEETS

SERVES 4

Harvard beets are as New England as Harvard University. The tangy and smooth sauce used here is a great complement to beets, which is probably why this recipe has been around forever. Put them on a big-game buffet table when entertaining folks who went to Yale or Princeton. They will be envious.

FOR THE BEETS
5 medium beets, trimmed
1 teaspoon white vinegar
1½ teaspoons salt

FOR THE SAUCE
1 tablespoon cornstarch
1½ tablespoons sugar
¼ teaspoon white pepper
¼ cup cider vinegar
1 tablespoon butter

For the beets: Put the beets in a large pot and add enough water to cover. Add the white vinegar and 1 teaspoon of the salt. Bring to a boil over high heat. Reduce heat to medium high to maintain the boil. Cook 1 hour or until fork-tender.

When cooked through, reserve ⅔ cup of the water, then drain the beets. Let the beets cool. When the beets are cool enough to handle, slip off the skins. Cut the beets into thick slices and set aside.

For the sauce: In a medium saucepan, combine the cornstarch, sugar, the remaining ½ teaspoon salt, and white pepper and whisk together. On low heat, whisk in the reserved beet water and the cider vinegar. Raise the heat to high and continue whisking until the sauce comes to a boil. Let boil about 1 minute, until the sauce has thickened. Reduce the heat to medium, stir the beets into the sauce, and cook about 5 minutes, or until the beets are warmed. Serve immediately.

30-YARD LINE SLAW

SERVES 8

This crisp and tasty slaw is great to bring to a cookout. The apple gives it a hint of sweetness, and the cider vinegar adds a nice punch. If you are pressed for time, go ahead and purchase the precut slaw blend in the salad section of the grocery store. But if you do have time, please slice your own cabbages; they will be much more flavorful.

½ head of green cabbage, halved, cored and thinly shredded
½ head of red cabbage, halved, cored, and thinly shredded
3 Gala, Honeycrisp, or Macoun apples, finely diced
½ cup dried cranberries
½ cup chopped walnuts
¼ cup chopped dates
¼ cup cider vinegar
1 cup mayonnaise
1 teaspoon salt
1 teaspoon pepper
Pinch of cinnamon

In a large bowl, combine the green and red cabbages, apples, cranberries, walnuts, and dates. Add the vinegar and toss until the cabbage mixture is evenly coated. Let wilt about 15 minutes, or until the cabbage has given off some liquid. In a small bowl, combine the mayonnaise, salt, pepper, and cinnamon.

Drain half of the liquid from the cabbage mixture. Stir in the mayonnaise mixture until the cabbage mixture is evenly coated. Refrigerate at least an hour, or until halftime. Serve cold.

IT WAS A DARK AND STORMY AFTERNOON

The official drink of Bermuda is the Dark and Stormy. It's also found in bars in sailing towns up and down the East Coast. It consists of two things: Gosling's Black Seal rum and ginger beer. Some people add a bit of lime juice, but that, of course, is up to you.

2 fluid ounces Gosling's Black Seal rum or any dark rum

3 fluid ounces ginger beer

Fill a highball glass halfway with ice cubes. Add the rum and ginger beer. Stir. Consume while you discuss the last silver you won!

SEVEN-LAYER BARS

SERVES 12

This treat could not be easier to put together. When I made them for a friend, she mentioned that she had the same recipe from an old church cookbook. The recipe must have been around for generations. My question is, where is the seventh layer? The answer seems to be the butter! No wonder the original recipe card had written on the bottom "eat and grow fat!"

½ cup butter, melted
1½ cups graham cracker crumbs
½ cup shredded coconut
6 ounces semisweet chocolate chips

6 ounces butterscotch chips
1 14-ounce can sweetened condensed milk
½ cup chopped walnuts

Preheat the oven to 325°F.

Pour the butter into a 9 x 9-inch glass baking dish. Add the graham cracker crumbs and press evenly into the bottom. Sprinkle the coconut evenly over the graham crackers, followed by the chocolate chips, butterscotch chips, and condensed milk. Sprinkle the chopped walnuts over the top.

Bake for 30 minutes, or until the chocolate has melted.

Let cool completely, and then cut into 12 bars.

SPORTY COCKTAILS

Different sports require different cocktails. Here are some cocktails that will suit your sporting occasion perfectly.

- Polo or Wimbledon: Pimm's Cup (page 77)
- Kentucky Derby: Mint Julep
- Sailing: Dark and Stormy (page 90)
- Golf: Arnold Palmer (add vodka, and call it a John Daly)
- Tennis: Gin and Tonic (for hydration; page 63)
- Crew: beer (preferably a good British Ale)
- Skiing: Hot Buttered Rum (page 243)
- Squash: Jack and ginger ale

THE PERFECT PICNIC

A picnic is a perfect preppy party: It takes place in the great outdoors, frequently near or on a body of water, and is reminiscent of a tailgate. Wine, beer, and, of course, gin and tonics just add to the fun. What could be better? Add a nice old wool blanket or two, a can of bug spray, and a cooler full of ice, and you're all set. It can be sporty (bring a badminton set), romantic (bring candles), or family-friendly (bring the kids, and don't forget the nanny).

SOME SAMPLE PICNIC BASKET FILLERS

- Cheese and crackers, preferably a nice hard cheddar, an aged gouda, and a box of Wheat Thins

- Chips and dip

- Green seedless grapes

- Marinated olives (page 74) served at room temperature

- Turkey and Havarti cheese sandwiches with cranberry mayo on Date Nut Bread (page 138)

- Cheese Twists with Olives (page 79)

- Lobster salad (page 43)

- New Potato Salad with Dill (page 45)

- Thermos filled with G and Ts

- Bottle of white wine, preferably a crisp Sancerre

- Twelve-pack of beer (keep it old school, just real beer)

- Plenty of ice

THE

GRAND

TOUR

In a perfect world (which in many cases is, indeed, the world of a prep), the perfect gift for a newly minted college grad is a few months in Europe to see the world and get some culture. The tour typically starts in England, purely because we speak the same language and so many of our people have roots across the pond. Traveling by rail, the trip can last anywhere from three weeks to a year. Of course, it helps if you have family or friends in places like Lake Como, Toulouse, or Capri. A distant cousin with an estate in England wouldn't hurt a smidge.

For some, however, traveling halfway round the world is just not that easy. And that is just fine. A trip to Astoria, Queens, can give a hint of life in Athens sans the Parthenon. Chinatown in San Francisco offers a world of flavor and culture. And a drive along Route 66 can be a real eye-opener. The following recipes are an eclectic blend of cultures and flavors.

PISSALADIÈRE

SERVES 4

Paris is a preppy must. After all, we all learned to speak French from the time we were twelve, and going to Paris is a chance to use that knowledge. Of course, drinking a nice white Burgundy makes the French words roll off the tongue a little easier and with a much better accent.

The pissaladière is an elegant variation of a French-style pizza. Using puff pastry instead of pizza dough elevates it to a plated appetizer that can be served at a formal dinner party.

Feel free to be creative. If you don't like anchovies, you could use a different thinly sliced meat. Like your pizza with cheese? You could add some. You can make a pissaladière any way you like.

1 large onion, thinly sliced
3 tablespoons butter
1 sheet puff pastry, lightly rolled out and
    cut into 3-inch squares

12 flat anchovies, whole
20 pitted kalamata olives

In a small sauté pan, sweat the onions in 2 tablespoons of the butter over low heat. Cook about 20 minutes, until the onions are almost soft enough to fall apart, but not browned. Reserve.

Place the puff pastry squares on a baking sheet. In another small sauté pan, melt the remaining 1 tablespoon butter over low heat. Brush onto the puff pastry squares.

Bake the puff pastry according to manufacturer's directions, until almost cooked but not yet golden brown. Remove from the oven and top with the onion, anchovies, and olives. Bake for 5 minutes more.

Serve immediately.

Note: If you can find fresh white anchovies, they are very delicate in flavor.

BIG '80s SALAD WITH GOAT CHEESE CROUTONS

SERVES 6

Based on the fun flavors of the preppy days of yore, this salad is filled with the tastes of that over-the-top decade. In the eighties, it seemed like sun-dried tomatoes and goat cheese were the big new things at every restaurant. Now, well, the ingredients in this salad are so well known that they're no big deal, just ingredients. I've combined all of these into a salad that is a treat and a taste of the days of the big eighties restaurants, like the Quilted Giraffe, the 21 Club, Lutèce, and Chanterelle. Consider it a little trip to New York City, circa 1987!

1 8-ounce log fresh goat cheese
¼ cup marinated sun-dried tomatoes
3 tablespoons balsamic vinegar
½ garlic clove
⅓ cup vegetable oil
1 teaspoon salt
1 teaspoon white pepper
¼ cup flour

1 egg
½ cup panko bread crumbs seasoned with ½ teaspoon salt and ¼ teaspoon white pepper
½ cup canola oil
1 head of frisée
¼ cup toasted pine nuts
½ cup pitted oil-cured olives

Cut the goat cheese into ¾-inch rounds. Place on a baking sheet and freeze for 30 minutes. (It's okay if the cheese rounds take up the space where the Absolut usually sits; removing the vodka from your freezer for 30 minutes won't hurt, and if you feel like it, mix up a quick Cosmopolitan to really channel the era.)

While the cheese is freezing, make the vinaigrette. In a blender, process the sun-dried tomatoes, vinegar, garlic, oil, salt, and white pepper on high for about two minutes until emulsified and the sun-dried tomatoes are fully broken down.

When the goat cheese is frozen and your Cosmo is finished, set up your dredging station. Spread the flour out on a plate. Beat the egg in a shallow dish. Spread the seasoned panko on a second plate. Working with 1 cheese round at a time, dredge in the flour, dip in egg, and then coat in the panko, pressing firmly to adhere. Repeat until all the cheese rounds are breaded.

Have a paper towel–lined plate ready next to the stove. In a large sauté pan, heat the oil over high heat. Carefully place the cheese rounds in the oil and fry for 1 minute. Flip and fry for a minute more, until just golden. Transfer to the paper towel–lined plate to drain.

In a large bowl, toss the frisée with the vinaigrette. Arrange the frisée on four plates. Top each with 2 goat cheese croutons, the pine nuts, and olives.

Serve immediately.

BELLINIS

A must-stop on any grand tour is the gorgeous city of Venice. It's way more fun to zip around in a vaporetto than a yellow cab. (Or, if you are like my friend and I, "borrow" a gondola that has caught your eye for the past three days.) This delightful little sparkling cocktail originated at Harry's Bar at Venice's famous Hotel Cipriani.

3 fluid ounces prosecco

1 ripe peach, pureed, or 2 fluid ounces peach nectar

In a mixing glass, combine the prosecco and the pureed peach. Stir and pour into a Champagne flute. Close your eyes and pretend you are looking at the Canal Grande. Repeat as many times as necessary until you close your eyes and believe you are looking at the Canal Grande.

WARM GERMAN POTATO SALAD

SERVES 6

I first tasted warm potato salad in Salzburg, yes, the home of a movie near and dear to every preppy's heart: *The Sound of Music.* Who doesn't love Julie Andrews and that voice? (She also played Mary Poppins, another preppy icon.) I was at a little restaurant that was actually in a tree house of all places, and this potato salad was served alongside schnitzel. (I expected noodles, but, hey, I could still sing about "My Favorite Things.") This recipe is a simple variation based on the first recipe for German potato salad I ever made—from a 1960s Betty Crocker cookbook.

2 pounds small new potatoes, scrubbed	1 tablespoon salt
6 slices bacon	½ teaspoon celery salt
1 large onion, finely diced	¼ teaspoon white pepper
2 tablespoons flour	¾ cup water
2 tablespoons sugar	⅓ cup cider vinegar

In a large pot, combine the potatoes with cold water to cover. Bring to a boil over high heat. Reduce the heat and cook for 15 to 20 minutes, or until the potatoes pierce easily with a fork. Immediately remove from the stove and put the pot under cold water. Let the potatoes fully cool.

While the potatoes are cooling, in a large sauté pan, cook the bacon over medium heat until crisp, turning frequently, about 15 minutes. Remove the bacon from the pan, leaving the bacon fat in the pan. Add the onions and lightly sauté for 5 minutes, until just translucent and cooked through. Stir in the flour, sugar, salt, celery salt, and white pepper and cook over low heat until it just begins to bubble. Whisk in the water and the vinegar, increase the heat to medium high and bring back to a boil. Whisk and boil for about 2 minutes more.

When the potatoes are cool enough to handle, cut them into quarters and place in a bowl. Pour the sauce over the potatoes and fold until combined. Crumble the bacon into the potato salad and fold until combined. Serve immediately.

A SPLURGE IN ITALY

I made my second big trip to Europe in the summer of 1988. I was with my then companion Tony, and we were headed to Italy. Young, with little money but lots of enthusiasm, we got off the plane in Rome and hit the ground running. Our first day and night was a splurge. We were staying in a very swank hotel on the Via Veneto and had picked out our first dinner from a real travel guide—a guide for well-heeled adults that were not on a budget—as opposed to the rest of our picks for the next three weeks, which were from *Let's Go* or *Italy on $20 a Day*. (Gosh, can you imagine going to Italy for $20 a day in this day and age? Lucky to get a pizza for that!)

After a long day of sightseeing, we arrived at the restaurant rather early for Roman dining—around seven thirty that evening. The restaurant was a small trattoria, down a steep flight of steps, in the basement. There were perhaps eight tables. Fresh pasta and herbs hung from the ceiling of the dining room to dry. In one corner was an antipasti table.

My goodness, this was Italy! We sat down and waited for the menu. What arrived was a handwritten card, in Italian, obviously, with a choice of three things: fish, veal, or chicken. That was it. A vino da tavola was placed in a jug on the table. The waiter pointed to the antipasti bar, which, if I recall, we treated like an all-you-can-eat buffet.

Then our meal arrived. I don't remember what I consumed, but it was delightful. Dessert and espresso followed. When we left, it was well after midnight and we had fallen in love with Italy.

I wish I had written down the name of the restaurant. Who knows if now, almost thirty years later, it still exists. I ran into Tony at my thirtieth high school reunion. After catching up for a few minutes, I looked at him and asked if he remembered that meal in Italy, because I thought it was one of the best meals of my life. He looked right at me and said he felt the same way. It was a meal worth remembering. What a memory it is!

GRILLED CHEDDAR AND BRANSTON PICKLE SANDWICHES

MAKES 1 SANDWICH

One of the niftiest condiments in all of England is the Branston Pickle. It is a unique savory and slightly tart spread. You can find it in any grocery store in the U.K. and, of course, at every pub. It is a major element of the quintessential ploughman's lunch. If you cannot find Branston Pickle in a store, you can make it. It tastes almost as good as the real thing!

2 slices pullman or sourdough bread
4 ounces English cheddar cheese, such as Five Counties

2 tablespoons Branston Pickle (recipe follows)
1 tablespoon butter

On the bread slices, spread the cheese and pickle. In a small sauté pan, melt the butter over medium heat. Place the sandwich in the pan and cook for about 3 minutes, until golden brown. Flip the sandwich and cook about 3 minutes more, until the other side is golden brown.

Cut the sandwich in half, on the diagonal, and serve.

BRANSTON PICKLE

MAKES ABOUT FIVE 1-PINT JARS

1 large carrot, diced
½ rutabaga, peeled and finely diced
3 garlic cloves, minced
4 dates, finely chopped
½ head of cauliflower, chopped
1 large onion, chopped
1 Granny Smith apple, chopped
2 zucchini, chopped
10 gherkins, chopped

½ cup packed dark brown sugar
1 teaspoon salt
2 tablespoons lemon juice
¾ cup malt vinegar
1½ teaspoons ground allspice
1 teaspoon mustard seeds
½ teaspoon cayenne pepper or chili powder

In stockpot, combine the carrot, rutabaga, garlic, dates, cauliflower, onion, apple, zucchini, gherkins, sugar, salt, lemon juice, vinegar, allspice, mustard seeds, and cayenne. Bring just to a boil. Reduce the heat to very low and simmer, uncovered, for about 2 hours, until the rutabaga is just soft. Add a little water as needed.

Let cool, and refrigerate in an airtight container for at least 2 days to allow the flavors to combine. Store in the refrigerator for up to 1 week. Or, can, like the pickle recipe on page 83.

SCALLOPS WITH BLOOD ORANGE-CREAM SAUCE

SERVES 4

Seared scallops are easy to cook, and even easier to overcook. Because they release sugar as you sear them, it is easy to get a lovely caramelized coating. In the dead of winter, when blood oranges are in season, it's nice to hark back to those lazy summer days of going clamming and scalloping at the Cape Cod house.

16 large day boat or dry scallops
¼ teaspoon salt, plus more as needed
¼ teaspoon black pepper
2 tablespoons butter
1 tablespoon olive oil
¼ cup juice of blood orange (or regular orange)

1 tablespoon white wine
1 tablespoon clam juice
1 tablespoon heavy cream
½ teaspoon vanilla extract
¼ teaspoon white pepper

Carefully pat the scallops dry with a paper towel. Season with the salt and black pepper.

In a large sauté pan, heat 1 tablespoon of the butter and the oil over very high heat. Heat until bubbling hot, then carefully place the scallops in the pan in a single uncrowded layer. Sear the scallops, without touching them or moving the pan, for about 1½ minutes, until the scallops easily release from the pan. Using tongs, carefully flip the scallops and cook for 1½ minutes more, until the other side is golden brown and easily releases from the pan. The scallops will be golden brown on the outside and nice and rare on the inside. Transfer the scallops to a warm plate.

Pour off the fat from the pan. Place the pan over medium heat. Add the blood orange juice, wine, and clam juice and cook for 2 minutes, until slightly reduced. Reduce the heat to low, add the cream and the remaining 1 tablespoon butter, and cook until the butter melts. Let the sauce reduce for 1 minute. Add the vanilla and white pepper and remove from the heat. Taste and add salt as needed.

Pour the sauce over the scallops and serve.

Note: Day boat scallops are the freshest available. Dry scallops have no water added and are fresh as well. Never use wet scallops to sear, it just will not do.

TARRAGON CHICKEN

SERVES 6

The cookbook I refer to again and again is Patricia Wells's stunning *At Home in Provence*. It has literally fallen apart from constant use; I had to buy a second copy. That has only happened to me once before, and that was with a record album (yep, a record and, yep, that was a long time ago). The same thing happened to Joni Mitchell's *Blue*. I wore it out. Yes, the book is that good. The first recipe that broke the binding on the book was her recipe for chicken with tarragon and sherry vinegar. I have made it literally hundreds of times. The recipe is perfect as is, but I found over the years that people actually don't like dark meat much, so I've adjusted and tweaked it slightly to accommodate only chicken breasts. I also I added a bit more tarragon, just because I love it so much.

⅓ cup flour
1 teaspoon salt
½ teaspoon white pepper
6 skin-on chicken breasts, rib bones removed
3 tablespoons butter
3 tablespoons olive oil
7 tablespoons sherry vinegar
3 large onions, thinly sliced

8 shallots, thinly sliced
10 garlic cloves, peeled and halved
2 cups chicken stock
1 generous bunch fresh tarragon
2 sprigs fresh rosemary
2 tablespoons tomato paste
1½ tablespoons Dijon mustard
¾ cup heavy cream

Preheat the oven to 350°F.

On a plate, stir together the flour, salt, and white pepper. Dredge the chicken in the seasoned flour, turning to coat both sides.

In a large Dutch oven or flameproof casserole dish, heat the butter and oil over high heat, until the butter-oil mixture is almost bubbling. Place the chicken, skin side down, in the pot. Reduce the heat to medium, and sear the chicken for about 8 minutes, until golden brown. Flip, and cook 4 minutes. Transfer the chicken, skin side up, to a platter. While the chicken rests, sprinkle 3 tablespoons of the vinegar on the chicken skin.

Pour off all but 3 tablespoons of the fat from the Dutch oven. Add the onions, shallots, and garlic and cook over medium heat about 10 minutes, until just slightly golden in color. Add ½ cup of the chicken stock to the onion mixture, and then return the chicken and its juices to the pot. Cover the chicken with all but one of the tarragon sprigs and the rosemary. Cover and bake for 35 minutes.

Transfer the chicken to a warmed platter, leaving the onion mixture in the dish. There will be a lovely sauce in the bottom of the pan. Discard the tarragon and rosemary. Stir in the tomato paste, mustard, and the remaining 4 tablespoons of vinegar. Add the remaining 1½ cups chicken stock, stir to combine, and bring the sauce to a boil. Reduce the heat to medium low and simmer for about 10 minutes, until the sauce is thickened. Reduce the heat to low and stir in the cream. Cook for 5 minutes more. Snip the remaining tarragon over the sauce.

Pour the sauce over the chicken and serve.

Pour a killer wine and toast Patricia Wells on this one!

GRILLED FLANK STEAK
WITH AUTHENTIC CHIMICHURRI SAUCE

SERVES 5-6

The recipe for this Argentinean sauce was given to me by my sous chef's mother, Patricia. She is a great, great cook, and her son made this sauce frequently at the restaurant.

FOR THE SAUCE
1 cup finely chopped fresh cilantro
1 cup finely chopped fresh parsley
2 garlic cloves, minced
Juice of 3 to 4 lemons (½ cup)
2 tablespoons water
1 tablespoon olive oil
1 teaspoon salt

FOR THE STEAK
1 1¾- to 2-pound flank steak
1 teaspoon salt
1 teaspoon pepper

For the sauce: Combine the cilantro, parsley, and garlic in a small bowl, stirring with a small spatula or fork. Squeeze in the lemon juice and add the water and oil. Mix well. Add the salt and check for seasoning. Reserve the sauce in the refrigerator until ready to serve.

For the steak: Preheat a gas grill to high heat or prepare a charcoal grill for direct grilling (see page 54).

Season the steak with the salt and pepper. Place the steak on the grill, and grill for about 4 minutes on each side, until medium-rare. Transfer the steak to a plate and let rest for 10 minutes.

Slice the steak thinly against the grain. Pour the sauce over the warm steak and serve immediately.

SAUSAGE ROLLS AND MEAT PIES

It was every gal's dream come true. I graduated college, and my parents' gift to me was a trip to Europe. Not only that, to make the dream better, I was going with just about the most handsome preppy man you could imagine. I will admit that at that point in my life, I had never used public transportation (and very rarely a public rest-room). They gave me an open-ended plane ticket that began in London and ended in Paris. Additionally, they gave me a certain amount of money to live on during that time. They assumed, with my lifestyle, that the money would last a whopping two weeks. Instead, it lasted more than three months.

With glee, I would send them postcards of my escapades. "Gee Mommy," I would write, "we've camped the last five nights. Thank goodness it rained. I stripped off my clothes and stood outside in the downpour and got to wash my hair." Or "Thanks for packing that wonderful first-aid kit. We needed it, as a sheep chewed a hole in our tent, and those Band-Aids really fixed the hole, since the rain was coming in."

This preppy gal lived a life I would love to live again. I hitchhiked. I rented a car smaller than my closet. I slept on sheep farms in Great Britain. I slept on trains, in strangers' homes, and in bed-and-breakfasts. One night, I slept in a rental car on the side of the road.

I saw and, I mean, really noticed, every detail of Europe. The first six weeks were spent in Great Britain. My WASPy roots were right there, and I felt like I was at home from the get-go.

The first thing I learned was how to eat cheap. Gosh, I miss those days, because eating cheap was eating well. There were all these little shops in small villages throughout the U.K. that served up two things that traveled well in a backpack: sau-sage rolls and meat pies. We ate them in the pouring rain, we ate them hitchhiking, we ate them driving, and we ate them sightseeing. To this day, if I bite into a good sausage roll or meat pie, I am 22 again, doing without a shower for three days, wear-ing the same L.L. Bean sweater that was my pillow the night before, and feeling like I was in heaven.

As an aside, a sausage roll is a lovely little snack. Simply cook an Irish banger or similar mild sausage. Wrap it up in puff pastry, brush it with a little well beaten egg and bake until golden. Yes, it is basically a giant pig in a blanket with a niftier name. Delish!

EASY BEEF STROGANOFF

SERVES 4 GENEROUSLY

Beef stroganoff sounds so international. Its roots are firmly in Russia, but it's now a dish that's made around the world. The creamy sauce is a bit reminiscent of cream of mushroom soup, so preps everywhere can eat it and still feel like Mommy made it. Serve the stroganoff over buttered egg noodles with chopped parsley for an authentic preparation.

Many years ago, when the USSR first allowed visitors, I immediately got a visa, and headed to Moscow and what was then Leningrad (in January, believe it or not!). It was quite the bargain at the time. The package was $600 for nine days, including airfare, tickets to the Bolshoi Ballet, the opera, a visit to the Summer Palace, and all meals. The minute we arrived, our passports and visas were taken. We could go absolutely nowhere without a guide. It was quite a lesson and oh so fascinating. However, not once was I offered stroganoff.

1 2½-pound beef tenderloin roast cut into ½-inch strips	3 tablespoons Cognac or brandy
2 teaspoons salt	1 cup beef broth or stock
2 teaspoons pepper	½ cup heavy cream
8 tablespoons butter	1 tablespoon Dijon mustard
⅓ cup onion or shallot, finely diced	½ cup sour cream
2 cups button mushrooms, halved	2 tablespoons chopped fresh dill
2 tablespoons flour	2 tablespoons Worcestershire sauce

Season the beef with the salt and pepper.

In a large heavy-bottomed skillet, melt 2 tablespoons of the butter over medium heat. Working in batches, cook the beef, making sure not to crowd the pan, about 1 minute on each side. Transfer to a bowl or rimmed platter.

Melt the remaining 6 tablespoons butter over medium eat. Add the onion and cook until translucent, scraping the bottom of the pan to get any of the remaining brown bits from the beef. Reduce the heat to medium low, and sauté the mushrooms in the butter-onion mixture for about 8 minutes, until lightly browned. Sprinkle the flour over the mushrooms and stir until combined.

Deglaze the pan with the Cognac, stirring, and immediately add the broth. Simmer stirring frequently, for 15 minutes, until the sauce thickens. Stir in the cream, the Worcestershire sauce, and mustard and simmer for 5 minutes more. Return the beef and its juices to the pan, and cook 2 to 4 minutes, until the beef is medium-rare.

Remove from the heat, and stir in the sour cream and dill. Season with salt and pepper to taste. Serve immediately.

BRAISED SHORT RIBS OF BEEF WITH ESPRESSO-CHOCOLATE GRAVY

SERVES 6

Yes, Braised Short Ribs with Espresso-Chocolate Gravy sounds a bit odd. But, really, it is not. Meat can be rubbed or marinated with espresso beans. This is a more refined way to infuse that flavor into the dish. The slightest hint of chocolate takes away a bit of the espresso's bitterness, creating a well-balanced sauce. At the restaurant, when we'd put this on as a special, we knew it would practically fly out the door.

- 2 tablespoons flour, plus more for dredging
- 2 teaspoons salt
- 2 teaspoons pepper
- 4 pounds beef short ribs, cut into 2-inch lengths
- ¼ cup vegetable oil
- 2 cups onions, thickly sliced
- 4 garlic cloves, peeled
- 3 large carrots, sliced into ½-inch rounds
- 3 stalks celery, cut into ½-inch slices
- 3 tablespoons tomato paste
- ¼ cup brewed espresso or coffee
- 3 cups beef broth, or veal, or chicken stock
- 3 bay leaves
- 2 to 4 tablespoons semisweet or bittersweet chocolate chips

Preheat the oven to 325°F.

On a plate, stir together the flour, salt, and pepper. Dredge the beef in the seasoned flour, turning to coat all sides.

In a large Dutch oven or covered flameproof casserole dish, heat the oil over high heat. When the oil is hot but not quite smoking, add the beef, and sear on all four sides about 4 minutes, until brown. Transfer to a plate.

Reduce the heat to medium, and add the onions, garlic, carrots, and celery and lightly sauté about 10 minutes, until the onions and garlic are golden but not burned. Add the tomato paste and cook until the paste turns a rust color, about 5 minutes, constantly scraping the bottom of the pan to get any of the remaining brown bits from the beef. Sprinkle the vegetable mixture with 2 tablespoons flour, incorporating it well.

Deglaze the pan with the espresso and immediately add the broth. Stir constantly, so that a gravy forms. Return the beef and its juices to the pan, bone side down, and raise the heat to high. Add the bay leaves and bring to a simmer, then remove from heat. Cover and braise for 1 hour.

Remove the pan from the oven, uncover, and stir, scraping the bottom to get any of the remaining brown bits from the beef. Cook the short ribs for 3 more hours, checking the liquid level occasionally to make sure the bottom does not burn and adding more water as needed.

Remove the pan from the oven, and let stand uncovered about 15 minutes. Skim any fat from the top of the pan. Transfer the ribs to a platter and cover lightly with foil.

Heat the pan over low heat and stir the gravy and vegetables. Taste and add salt and pepper as needed. Stir in 2 tablespoons of the chocolate. Taste and add up to 2 tablespoons more chocolate to taste. Remove the bay leaves.

Spoon the gravy and vegetables over the beef and serve.

Note: Ask your butcher to cut the short ribs into 2-inch lengths.

MOUSSAKA

SERVES 12-14

own the street from where I grew up was the most delightful neighbor. Fran was from Greece and she was just about the best home cook I knew. Her church would have a food festival every year, and my family would go and eat all of her wonderful Greek specialties. I finagled this moussaka recipe from Fran, as her moussaka rivals any I have enjoyed in Greece. Fair warning, this recipe is complicated, time-consuming, and rich! However, it is well worth the effort. It serves a crowd, so plan a dinner party around it. You will be lauded for your international je ne sais quoi.

3 large eggplants
2 quarts water
½ cup salt
Flour for dredging
1 cup olive oil (not extra-virgin)
6 tablespoons butter
3 cups finely chopped sweet onions
2 garlic cloves, minced
1½ pounds ground beef, such as chuck
1½ pounds ground lamb
2 cups tomato sauce

2 bay leaves
Pinch of oregano
2 cups dry red wine
½ teaspoon ground cinnamon
2 tablespoons chopped fresh parsley
Salt and pepper to taste
10 button mushrooms, trimmed and thinly sliced
1½ quarts Béchamel Sauce (page 118)
1 cup grated Romano cheese

Cut the eggplants crosswise into ½-inch slices. Transfer to a large bowl and cover with the water and salt. Let stand for 20 minutes, then drain. Rinse the eggplant under cold water and pat dry with paper towels.

Spread the flour on a plate. Dredge the eggplant slices in the flour, turning to coat both sides.

Have a paper towel–lined baking sheet or a wire rack next to the stove. In a large sauté pan, heat the oil over high heat. Add the eggplant, and cook quickly on both sides, about 2 minutes, until golden brown. Transfer the eggplant to the prepared baking sheet.

In a large skillet, heat 4 tablespoons of the butter and cook the onions about 5 minutes, until translucent. Add the garlic and cook 1 minute, until just golden brown. Add the beef and lamb and cook, stirring and breaking them up with a wooden spoon, about 7 minutes, until lightly browned. Add the tomato sauce, bay leaves, oregano, wine, cinnamon, parsley, salt, and pepper, and simmer until almost all of the liquid is absorbed.

(Continued on page 118)

While the meat sauce is simmering, in a sauté pan over high heat, cook the mushrooms in the remaining 2 tablespoons butter for 5 minutes, until golden. Add to the meat sauce. Preheat the oven to 400°F.

Generously butter a 12 x 16 x 2-inch lasagna or roasting pan and arrange half of the eggplant on the bottom. Add the meat mixture and top with the remaining eggplant. Pour the Béchamel Sauce on top and sprinkle with the cheese. Bake, uncovered, for 1 hour, until golden.

Let stand for 40 minutes, then cut into squares and serve.

BÉCHAMEL SAUCE

This béchamel sauce is enriched with egg to help keep the Moussaka together. Normally, there are no eggs in béchamel sauce.

4 tablespoons butter
¼ cup flour
5 cups whole milk
6 eggs

1 cup heavy cream
1 tablespoon ground nutmeg
2 teaspoons salt

In a saucepan, melt the butter over low heat. Add the flour and cook, whisking constantly, for 2 minutes. Add the milk and cook, whisking constantly. Let simmer on low heat for 20 minutes, stirring frequently. Turn off the heat and let cool slightly.

In a large bowl, beat the eggs. Stir in the heavy cream. Add a bit of the warm milk sauce to temper the cream-egg mixture. Then add the cream-egg sauce to the milk mixture. Stir to combine, add nutmeg and salt, and stir again.

BRAISED ROMAINE LETTUCE
WITH BACON

SERVES 4

I know, I know! Lettuce is boring, and is served chilled, as a salad with other ingredients to liven it up. Romaine is just terrific as a Caesar. Why mess with greatness? Try this and perhaps you will have a different mind-set. A classic French preparation of lettuce, it is flavorful, and a nice change from the usual leafy green of spinach or Swiss chard. Serve with roasted meat.

- 4 heads of romaine lettuce, rinsed
- 4 slices bacon
- 1 tablespoon plus 1 teaspoon butter
- 1 shallot, minced
- 1½ cups low-sodium chicken stock or homemade chicken stock
- ¼ cup white wine
- ½ teaspoon pepper

Horizontally wrap each romaine head with a piece of bacon, securing it by tying the bacon in a knot. In a large Dutch oven or very deep sauté pan, melt 1 tablespoon of the butter over medium heat. Add the romaine and cook for 6 to 7 minutes, until wilted and slightly brown on all sides, being careful not to scorch.

Add the shallot, stock, and wine and bring to a boil. Reduce the heat to low and simmer for 30 minutes, uncovered, until almost all of the liquid has absorbed and the romaine leaves are fork-tender through the center.

Transfer the lettuce to a warm platter. There should be a thin film of buttery liquid in the pan. Add the pepper, the remaining 1 teaspoon of butter and warm over low heat until the butter melts. Pour the butter sauce over the lettuce and serve immediately.

SALMON WITH MARTINI SAUCE

SERVES 4

almon is a ubiquitous fish, seen in every fish store and on every restaurant menu. However, if you spend a bit more money, and are very picky about quality, salmon can be elevated to a precious protein. Ask your fishmonger to procure salmon that is wild caught and in season, such as Chinook or Sockeye. Almost all East Coast salmon is farmed and basically flavorless.

If you combine the wild salmon with the flavors of a martini, well, that is all that needs to be said.

4 6-ounce salmon fillets (high-quality seasonal wild-caught salmon)	½ cup veal stock (page 248)
¾ teaspoon salt	¼ cup gin
Pinch of black pepper	1 tablespoon butter
3 tablespoons olive oil	12 martini olives (pimento stuffed)
1 tablespoon dry vermouth	¼ teaspoon white pepper

Season the salmon with ¼ teaspoon of the salt and a pinch of black pepper.

In a large sauté pan, heat the oil over medium heat. Place the salmon, skin side up, in the pan and sauté for about 3 minutes. Carefully flip the salmon, and cook 2 to 3 minutes more, until the center is still nice and pink (for medium-rare). Transfer the salmon to a warmed platter.

Pour off the fat from the pan. Over low heat, deglaze the pan with the vermouth, then add the veal stock and gin. Raise the heat to medium-high and add the olives, the remaining ½ teaspoon salt, and the white pepper. Let the sauce simmer for about 2 minutes, until slightly reduced. Taste and add more salt and pepper as needed.

Pour the sauce over the salmon and serve.

Note: The homemade veal stock on page 248 comes to good use in this recipe. The veal stock adds a richness and mouth feel that cannot be substituted. If you do not make veal stock, then buy a high-quality demi-glace such as D'Artagnan, available by mail order.

FILET MIGNON WITH MOREL MUSHROOM SAUCE

SERVES 4

For years now, I forage morel mushrooms every spring. These wild mushrooms are odd looking and impossible to see, unless you are determined to find them. The morel pops up in the woods under rotting leaves that are in just the right condition. I have a secret spot where I go, and every year I come home with a brown bag filled with them. My favorite way to serve morels is with a cream sauce on bread. I also use a variation of that cream sauce and serve it with filet mignon.

1 cup morel mushrooms
4 6-ounce filet mignon steaks, room
   temperature
Salt and pepper to taste
½ tablespoon butter

½ large shallot, minced
¼ cup good-quality dry sherry
¼ cup good-quality beef, chicken, or
   veal stock (page 248)
½ cup heavy cream

Preheat the oven to 350°F.

Carefully cut each mushroom in half and remove any dirt with a soft slightly damp cloth.

Season the filets generously with salt and pepper. In a heavy-bottomed pan with an ovenproof handle, sear each side.

Transfer the pan with the filets to the oven, and cook about 5 minutes for rare, or 8 minutes for medium-rare. Transfer the filets to a platter and cover with foil.

While the filets cook, in a small sauté pan, melt the butter over high heat. When the butter is rather brown, add the morels and sear them nicely until they are golden brown.

Add the shallot and sauté for 1 minute and pour in the sherry to deglaze the pan.

Add the stock and cook for 5 minutes, until it reduces and the morels are soft.

Reduce the heat to low and add the cream. Cook for 10 minutes, until the sauce is reduced by half. Season with salt and pepper.

Pour the sauce over the filets and serve.

"AFTER EIGHT MINT" ICE CREAM

When my mom bought After Eight Mints, I knew she was having company. She would set them on the coffee table as a nibble during after-dinner drinks. Years and years later, I was designing a retro menu for a dinner party and thought of those mints and bought a box. I decided to make ice cream out of them, and it was a big success.

2 cups heavy cream
1 cup whole milk
⅓ cup sugar
2 tablespoons finely chopped fresh mint

2 tablespoons green crème de menthe
8 ounces After Eight Thin Mints, frozen
   and coarsely chopped

In a small saucepan with a lid, combine the cream, milk, and sugar over low heat. Bring just to a simmer and whisk vigorously, until the sugar is melted. Add the mint and the crème de menthe and stir to combine. Turn off the heat and cover the saucepan. Let cool, covered, about 1 hour.

Strain the mixture through a fine-mesh sieve placed over a large bowl. Cover and refrigerate at least 2 hours and up to 24 hours.

Pour the ice cream base into an ice cream maker, and freeze according to the manufacturer's instructions. When the ice cream is just beginning to freeze, slowly add the mints.

Serve immediately, or freeze for up to 4 days in a freezer-safe container.

GINGER CRINKLES

MAKES ABOUT 5 DOZEN COOKIES

nuggled up in front of a fire, curled up with a good book, a nice hot cup of tea, or a glass of warm milk, these cookies are as comforting as an old Hudson Bay point blanket.

2 cups flour
2 teaspoons baking soda
½ teaspoon salt
1 teaspoon ground cinnamon
2 teaspoons ground ginger

⅔ cup vegetable oil
1½ cups sugar
1 egg
½ cup molasses

Preheat oven to 350°F.

In a large bowl, sift together the flour, baking soda, salt, cinnamon, and ginger.

Using a standing mixer fitted with the paddle attachment, beat the oil, 1 cup of the sugar, and the egg on low speed until incorporated. Add molasses and increase speed and beat until all ingredients are combined.

Reduce the speed to low and gradually add the flour mixture, beating until well combined.

Spread the remaining ½ cup sugar out on a plate. To form each cookie, roll a teaspoon of dough into a ball, and roll the ball in the sugar. Place the cookies 2 inches apart on the baking sheet.

Bake the cookies one sheet at a time for 8 minutes, until the top has a slight split. Transfer to a wire rack to cool completely.

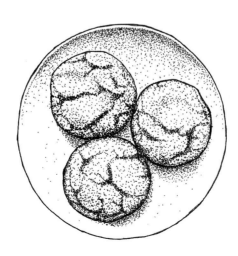

BRUNCH

AS A

VERB

Sunday brunch is perhaps the most important meal of the weekend for my people. It is a sure cure for early-morning hangovers as well as a social must, which require Bellinis, Bloodies, or, at worst, mimosas. Preppies know there's nothing quite like a Sunday afternoon party. It allows the drinking from Saturday night to continue with barely a break.

SMOKED SALMON AND BOURSIN QUICHE

SERVES 6-8

What's a nice brunch without a quiche? Still, I have had some quiches that sat in my stomach like lead. The reason: Too many eggs make the quiche more like a frittata in a pastry shell. The swell thing about this recipe is that it is light and airy, something a tummy recovering from a Saturday night will truly appreciate. The egg and cream mixture creates a custard, the smoked salmon adds a nice bit of flavorful protein, and the Boursin cheese contributes a touch of creamy elegance. Additionally, this quiche comes together very quickly; while it cooks, you can shower, dress, mix a Bloody, and be ready when your guests arrive.

3 eggs
1¾ cups heavy cream
1 teaspoon chopped fresh dill
½ teaspoon salt
¼ teaspoon white pepper

1 store-bought 9-inch frozen deep-dish pie shell
¼ pound Nova or Scottish-style smoked salmon, diced (see Note)
1 5.2-ounce Boursin garlic and herb cheese

Preheat the oven to 375°F.

In a medium bowl, whisk the eggs vigorously, until fluffy. Whisk in the cream, dill, and salt, and white pepper until fully incorporated.

Pour the mixture into the pie shell. Sprinkle the salmon evenly over the egg mixture, and top with dollops of Boursin.

Bake for 40 minutes, until just set. If the quiche is not lightly set, bake 5 minutes more. Let stand for 20 minutes before serving.

Note: Do not add the salmon and Boursin before pouring the egg mixture into the shell, or they will get stuck on the bottom of the pie shell.

AUNT ANNA'S CRANBERRY BREAD

MAKES 1 LOAF

No brunch table is complete without a few baked goods. I am a self-admitted baking-phobe; all that exact measuring scares me a bit. Will it rise? Will it burn? Will an Entenmann's cake suffice? My dear departed aunt Anna, who lived in Maine and had plenty of time on her hands to do a whole lot of baking, gave me this recipe years ago. It's foolproof. I've copied it exactly from her recipe card, right down to the method. If I could figure it out as an eighteen-year-old, I am positive I can't write it any better now.

2 cups flour
1 cup sugar
1½ teaspoons baking powder
½ teaspoon baking soda
1 teaspoon salt
¼ cup shortening or butter, cut into small pieces, plus butter for the loaf pan

¾ cup orange juice
1 tablespoon orange zest
1 egg, beaten
½ cup chopped walnuts or pecans
2 cups fresh cranberries, chopped

Preheat the oven to 350°F. Generously butter a 9 x 5 x 3-inch loaf pan.

In a large bowl, sift together the flour, sugar, baking powder, baking soda, and salt. Using two knives, cut the shortening into the flour mixture until the mixture resembles coarse cornmeal.

In a medium bowl, stir together the orange juice, orange zest, and egg. Pour all at once into the flour mixture, stirring just enough to dampen. Carefully stir in the nuts and cranberries.

Spoon the batter into the prepared loaf pan. With a spatula, spread the corners and sides slightly higher than center. Bake for about 1 hour, until the crust is golden brown and a toothpick inserted in the center comes out clean. Remove bread from the pan and let cool completely. Wrap in plastic wrap and store overnight for easy slicing.

BAKED EGGS FOR A CROWD

SERVES 12

I love a good eggs Benedict. But what I hate is when it is served on a buffet. The eggs are usually dried out or cold, the English muffin soggy, and the Canadian bacon dry. Similar to a Benedict, this method allows you to cook the eggs all at once and serve them in a neat little package. You can just pop the baked eggs out of the muffin tins and serve, with toast points and Hollandaise Sauce (page 140) on the side.

¼ cup butter, softened, for the muffin tin
12 slices ham
12 eggs

1 tablespoon assorted fresh herbs of your choice, such as basil, thyme, and chives
Salt and pepper to taste

Preheat the oven to 375°F.

Generously butter a 12-muffin tin. Carefully lay 1 ham slice in the bottom of each buttered cup, letting the edges fall over the top. Add 1 egg to each cup, being careful not to break the yolks. Sprinkle the eggs with the herbs and salt and pepper.

Bake 11 minutes, until the whites are set, but the yolk is runny. Let cool slightly, about 2 minutes. To transfer the eggs, carefully lift each one out using your fingers and place on a warm platter. Serve immediately.

BLOODIES

MAKES I PITCHER (ABOUT 5 CUPS)

Also known as "the cure," the Bloody should be consumed in the late morning to early afternoon. By three o'clock, move on to something else.

There are endless variations on the Bloody Mary. Some make it with tomato juice, some with V8, still others with Clamato. Regardless of the rendition, it must be served at brunch, as a nod to your fellow preps that you know they are probably showing up with a hangover. Imagine a world without Bloodies: Brunch would have a bunch of green-around-the-gills guests, milling around, not sure they can manage to choke down a piece of smoked salmon and not quite sure what they are doing at brunch in the first place.

With Bloodies, you'll have a lively bunch of guests, telling tales of their antics from the night before, gesturing wildly and happily, and ready to hit the buffet. Make a few pitchers; they will be consumed quickly.

1 quart Clamato
1 cup good-quality vodka
Juice of 2 large lemons
1 tablespoon clam juice
1 teaspoon Worcestershire sauce
1 teaspoon prepared horseradish
8 dashes of Tabasco sauce
1 teaspoon Old Bay Seasoning
Salt and pepper to taste
Garnish of your choice (below)

In a large pitcher, stir together the Clamato and the vodka. Add the lemon juice, clam juice, Worcestershire, horseradish, Tabasco, Old Bay and salt and pepper, tasting for flavor as you go.

Refrigerate for 1 hour. To serve, fill highball glasses halfway with ice cubes and pour the Bloodies over the ice.

Note: You can make the mix the day before serving, and add vodka when ready to consume.

GARNISHES FOR BLOODIES

Celery stalk
Stuffed green olives
Blanched haricot vert
Blanched asparagus
Gherkin
Scallion
Fresh raw clam (if using clam juice)
Radish peel
Lemon wedge
Cocktai shrimp

FRENCH TOAST WITH CARAMELIZED BANANAS AND WALNUTS

SERVES 10-12 PEOPLE, AS PART OF A BUFFET

decadent dish for a buffet or a holiday feast, this French toast can be made a day in advance and then reheated in the morning. That gives you time to concentrate on more important party tasks, like opening the Champagne or filling the ice buckets. The cream in the sauce helps balance the sweetness of the maple syrup. I count on serving half a piece of toast per guest, because, indeed, it is rich.

FOR THE TOASTS
8 eggs
½ cup whole milk
1 tablespoon sugar
1 teaspoon salt
8 ½-inch-thick slices brioche or challah bread (white will do in a pinch), sliced ½ inch thick
4 tablespoons butter

FOR THE SAUCE
4 tablespoons butter
3 ripe bananas, sliced
½ cup heavy cream
¼ cup maple syrup
1 tablespoon lemon juice
¾ cup walnut pieces

For the toasts: Preheat the oven to 350°F. Set a wire rack on a baking sheet.

In a medium bowl, whisk together the eggs, milk, sugar, and salt. Working with 1 slice of bread at a time, dip into the egg mixture and transfer to the rack.

In a large nonstick sauté pan, melt the butter over medium heat. Working in batches, sauté the bread, making sure not to crowd the pan, about 3 minutes on each side, until golden brown. Transfer to the rack. When all the slices are golden brown, place the rack with the toasts in the oven and cook 5 minutes more.

For the sauce: In a large sauté pan, melt the butter over low heat. Add the bananas, raise the heat to medium high, and cook until golden brown, about 5 minutes. When all the bananas are golden in color, add the cream and the syrup and reduce the heat to medium. Cook until the mixture is reduced by half; it should be thick and easily coat a wooden spoon. Stir in the lemon juice. Just before serving, stir in the walnuts. Spoon over toasts.

If making the day before: Transfer the toasts to a casserole dish, cover with plastic wrap and store in the refrigerator overnight. When ready to serve, warm them in a 350°F oven for about 10 minutes or until hot. In a large saucepan, reheat the sauce on low heat about 10 minutes until warm. Be careful to use low heat so the sauce does not separate.

A NICE JEWISH BRUNCH

While many preps are nibbling on bacon at brunch, our Jewish neighbors are having a much tastier brunch, but with a lot fewer Bloodies and a lot more food.

A Jewish brunch is just delicious. It usually includes dairy, which means there are no meats of any kind on the table to comply with kosher laws. A good Jewish brunch includes "Nova" (smoked Nova Scotia salmon, as opposed to the saltier belly lox); whitefish salad; chubs (a small smoked whitefish) or smoked sable; bagels; flavored cream cheese; a platter of sliced tomatoes, red onions, and cheeses; and a variety of delicious fruit and cheese pastries. The beverages would be juices, as opposed to vodka with juice in it.

For me, I prefer a good bagel with a smear of whitefish salad, a pile of Nova, and tomato slices. And I always wash it down with a Bloody.

Interesting smoked fish to try:

- Smoked trout
- Smoked sable
- Smoked haddock
- Kippers (very prep)
- Smoked mackerel
- Finnan haddock
- Smoked sturgeon

HANGOVER HASH BROWNS

SERVES 12 ON A BUFFET

A must at a casual brunch, this dish is loaded with all the culinary hangover remedies: starch, fat, and salt. If you plan to indulge the night before, assemble this dish and bake it in the morning. One might consider it "white trash cuisine," but heck, our people sometimes relish a bit of that.

2 pounds frozen hash browns
1 cup diced onion
1 pound sour cream
1 10¾-ounce can cream of chicken soup

8 tablespoons butter, melted
8 ounces grated sharp cheddar cheese
Crushed potato chips to taste

Remove the hash browns from the freezer and let thaw for 30 minutes.

In a large mixing bowl, combine the hash browns, onion, sour cream, cream of chicken soup, butter, and cheese. Pour the hash brown mixture into a 9 x 13-inch baking dish.

Bake for 1 hour. Scatter the potato chips on top and bake for 5 minutes more, until the chips are golden brown. Serve immediately.

WHAT TIME ARE WE EATING?

The timing of brunch is key. Too early, and your guests will simply decline the invitation, because preps are always prompt, and 11:30 on a Sunday morning is just out of the question. Once the time is too far past noon, well, that is a faux pas because too much time has passed nursing a hangover without the hair of the dog. Call the brunch for 12:15 and your guests will all arrive hungry, thirsty, and able to open their eyes.

DATE NUT BREAD

MAKES 1 LOAF

ell Nobel, a family friend in Maine, was known throughout town for her perfect breads. Her recipe for date nut bread is so old that I can see it was written with a fountain pen (or perhaps a feather!).

Serve it with a little cream cheese or use it for tea sandwiches.

1 8-ounce package chopped dates, such
    as Dromedary
1 teaspoon baking soda
1 cup boiling water
1 cup sugar
½ cup Crisco, other shortening, or butter,
    room temperature

1 egg
1½ teaspoons vanilla extract
1½ cups flour
½ teaspoon salt
½ cup chopped walnuts

Preheat the oven to 375°F.

Cut the dates into small pieces and put in a medium bowl. Add the baking soda and stir to coat the dates. Pour the boiling water over the mixture. Set aside.

Using a standing mixer fitted with the paddle attachment, beat the sugar with the Crisco on medium speed until well combined. Add the egg and the vanilla and cream until fluffy.

Sift the flour and salt into the egg mixture and beat until combined. Fold in the dates and walnuts.

Pour into a 8 x 5-inch loaf pan. Bake for 25 minutes, until a toothpick inserted in the center comes out clean. Bake 5 minutes more, if needed, and check again. Remove bread from the pan and let cool completely.

Wrap in plastic wrap and store overnight for easy slicing.

EASY AND PERFECT HOLLANDAISE

MAKES ½ CUP

When I was training at the Culinary Institute of America, hollandaise was one of those recipes that got under everybody's skin. First you would clarify butter, then set up a double boiler, it just went on and on. Then one day, I was watching an old video of Julia Child making hollandaise. First of all, that woman goes down as an icon of preppydom. A California WASP, transported to Paris, makes a huge mark in the cooking world like no other. I've done it her way ever since, and I will say that practice makes perfect. Buy a couple dozen eggs and a few pounds of butter the first few times—you just may need it. But practice, it does make perfect.

2 tablespoons white wine vinegar
3 egg yolks
8 tablespoons cold butter, cut into 8 pieces

Juice of ½ lemon
3 dashes of Tabasco sauce
Salt and white pepper to taste

Put the vinegar in a very heavy-bottomed small saucepan (and I mean a really heavy bottom), and cook over low heat about 5 minutes, until there is only a hint of vinegar in the pan. If you want to be all sorts of fancy, there is a term for this, called "reducing to au sec." Turn off the heat and transfer the saucepan immediately to a cool surface. Let the pan completely cool, about 10 minutes.

Add the egg yolks to the cool pan and, as Julia so perfectly put it, "beat them into submission." Indeed, whisk them until they are a bright yellow and thickened up a bit. Use some elbow grease.

Now, turn on a burner to medium heat. Put the pan on the burner and whisk those yolks. As soon as the pan gets a bit warm, remove it from the heat, and add 1 tablespoon of butter. Don't let the eggs scramble. Keep placing the pan on and off the heat as the butter melts. Add the remaining butter 1 tablespoon at a time in the same manner. Never stop whisking.

Once the hollandaise is thick enough to coat a spoon (you may need all the butter, you may not), transfer it to a small bowl. Add the lemon juice, Tabasco, and salt and pepper to taste.

Serve immediately.

A little hint: If the sauce begins to break (the butter and the eggs separate), add a dash of boiling water. It might fix it, then again, it might not. That's why you've got plenty of eggs and butter on hand.

SALMON SIDE IN THE STYLE OF LADIES OF THE EVENING

SERVES 12-14 ON A BUFFET

At one of my first cooking jobs, I was tasked with turning the less than desirable sides of salmon into something eye-appealing that could be sold for double the price of the raw fish. Eager to please, I came up with this rather simple salmon topping based on the Italian puttanesca sauce.

Over the years, I've served this dish at hundreds of brunches and luncheons. It always gets rave reviews. The trick, of course, is a nice fresh side of salmon. The other trick is to make sure it has cooled completely before you attempt to move it to a platter.

1 6- to 7-pound side of salmon, preferably wild, but if not, farmed will do
4 large garlic cloves
1 cup sun-dried tomatoes
2 yellow bell peppers, finely diced
Zest and juice of 2 large lemons
½ cup capers, rinsed

½ cup finely chopped fresh parsley
1 cup pitted kalamata olives
¼ cup olive oil
2 teaspoons coarsely ground black pepper
¾ cup dry white wine
¼ cup warm water

Preheat the oven to 400°F.

Line a jelly roll pan or rimmed baking sheet with parchment paper. Place the salmon, skin side down, on the prepared pan.

In a food processor, combine the garlic and sun-dried tomatoes, pulsing until finely chopped. Transfer to a large bowl.

Add the bell peppers, lemon zest, capers, parsley, and olives to the bowl and stir until combined. Stir in the lemon juice and oil, until a spreadable paste forms.

Evenly spread the paste on top of the salmon and season with the black pepper. (There's no need for salt thanks to the olives and capers.)

Pour the wine and water, carefully around the salmon, into the pan.

Bake for 17 minutes, until the salmon is just beginning to flake. Cool for 30 minutes, until the salmon is firm and cool enough to transfer.

Transfer to a platter. Serve at room temperature.

ENDIVE SALAD BUNDLES

SERVES 6

One of the troubles at a buffet is that there is a whole lot of food and not all that much room on your plate. And a green salad can take up a lot of that real estate. These simple salad bundles help solve that problem. They are small and tidy, and when opened, the salad tumbles out in a pretty little display. While admittedly tedious to make, the task is well worth the effort.

5 Belgian endives
1 cup mixed spring greens
¼ cup shredded carrot

¼ cup Balsamic Vinaigrette (recipe follows)
14 chives

Carefully select 30 of the largest, best-looking endive leaves and set aside. Finely chop the remaining endive leaves.

In a large bowl, combine the chopped endive, the greens, and carrot. Toss lightly with the Balsamic Vinaigrette.

To assemble the bundles, lay down 18 of the most uniform sized endive leaves on a work surface and top with a small amount of the greens mixture. Carefully stack one stuffed endive on top of another. Add a third stuffed endive next to the stacked ones. Tie the bundles carefully with 2 chives. Continue with the remaining ingredients, until 4 packages are assembled. Serve on a platter, with additional dressing on the side

---

Note: You will have some leftover endive leaves at the end. Use them the next day in a salad or with the hors d'oeuvres recipes on page 172.

BALSAMIC VINAIGRETTE

MAKES ABOUT 1 CUP

¼ cup best-quality balsamic vinegar
½ cup olive oil
1 tablespoon sugar

1 tablespoon finely chopped garlic
½ teaspoon salt
½ teaspoon pepper

In a jar with a tightly fitting lid, combine the vinegar, oil, sugar, garlic, salt, and pepper. Shake for 3 minutes, until thoroughly combined.

Refrigerate for up to 2 weeks in a sealed container.

VARIATIONS on EGGS BENEDICT

Once you have mastered hollandaise sauce, there are a variety of ways to serve it with eggs Benedict.

But first, you must master the perfect poached egg, which is not as easy as it seems. There are a few tricks to poaching eggs. First of all, make sure you have a big slotted spoon and a plate with plenty of paper towels lining it to drain the cooked egg. Second, you should be able to put your finger in the water and not scald it. If you have a nifty instant-read thermometer, and I hope you do, the water should be at 170°F.

Add about 1 teaspoon of distilled white vinegar to every 1 cup of water you warm up (you can be approximate here). How much water? Well, if the pan is a nonstick skillet, about 1½ inches deep; if you're using a pot, well, then 3 inches will do the trick. Most important, I ease the eggs into the water by first cracking them into a ladle and adding them to the poaching water that I have swirled around a bit with a spatula.

Don't crowd the eggs in the pan. It's better to cook a few at a time and just quickly warm them in the water again just before serving.

How long to cook them depends on how runny you want them. For me, about 4 minutes does the trick. I like my whites fully cooked and my yolks nice and runny.

When you remove the eggs, transfer them with the above-mentioned slotted spoon to the paper towel–lined plate.

Once you've mastered the poached egg, well, let the fun begin! Note that all the following variations use 1 poached egg per half muffin or piece of toast:

- **Eggs Benedict:** ½ buttered English muffin, grilled or griddled Canadian bacon, hollandaise
- **Eggs Florentine:** ½ buttered English muffin, sautéed spinach, hollandaise
- **Reuben Benedict:** Buttered rye toast, hollandaise with Dijon to taste stirred in, corned beef, Swiss cheese
- **Filet Benedict:** Buttered English muffin, thin slices of medium-rare filet mignon, béarnaise sauce (hollandaise with tarragon and tarragon vinegar, also known as sauce béarnaise)
- **Eggs Oscar:** Buttered English muffin, lump crabmeat, hollandaise
- **Veggie:** Buttered whole-wheat toast, sautéed mushrooms, blanched asparagus, hollandaise

PIGS IN A POKE

SERVES 6-8

Every brunch needs its fair share of pork products, and this pudding-like casserole does the perfect trick at a casual event. I serve it directly from the casserole dish that it bakes in. If you can find nice little Irish bangers, I recommend them, although any small breakfast sausage link will do just fine.

1 pound breakfast sausage links, such as
   Irish bangers
2 eggs, beaten

1 cup whole milk
1 cup flour, sifted
½ teaspoon salt

Preheat the oven to 400°F.

In a 7 x 11½-inch casserole or a 10-inch round cast-iron pan, arrange the sausages evenly. Pop into the oven for about 8 minutes, until the fat renders.

While the sausages are cooking, make the batter. In a large bowl, combine the eggs and milk. Add the flour and salt, and stir until combined.

Remove the sausages from the oven and raise the oven temperature to 475°F.

Pour the batter over the sausages into the casserole dish and bake for 8 minutes.

Reduce the heat to 350°F and bake 25 minutes more, until golden and the pudding is crispy on top and moist around the sausages.

Cut into squares and serve immediately.

RASPBERRY ALMOND
BRIE TART

SERVES 8

When I first opened Picnic, we needed a pastry chef. Until we found one, my sous chef Javier stepped up to the plate and started making dessert. He came up with this dish, which wound up being not only a sweet yet savory dessert at the restaurant, but a staple at our brunch catering events. The ubiquitous "Brie en croute" is reversed here and turned into a lovely tart that can be plated rather than spread on bread. The puff pastry, brushed with brandy, butter, and sugar, adds a touch of decadence.

More important, it is really quick and easy to make. You can assemble it ahead of time and simply save the last step (melting the Brie) until it is time to serve. While you can make the raspberry preserve a day or two before, it works just fine with a high-quality jarred jam.

½ cup butter
½ cup sugar
1 tablespoon brandy
½ tablespoon vanilla extract
1 sheet puff pastry

1½ cups Raspberry Jam (recipe follows) or best quality jarred jam
2 cups sliced almonds, lightly toasted
¾ pound Brie, softened

Preheat the oven to 375°F. Butter a jelly roll pan or rimmed baking sheet.

In a small saucepan, melt the butter with the sugar, brandy, and vanilla over low heat.

Lightly roll out the puff pastry and poke holes in it with a fork. Transfer to the prepared pan. Brush the pastry with the brandy butter. Bake for 10 to 15 minutes, until golden brown. Let cool. Do not turn the oven off.

In the meantime, if you choose, make the raspberry jam.

Spread the jam over the puff pastry, leaving the outer ½ inch uncovered, creating a border. Scatter the almonds over the jam.

Slice the Brie lengthwise and remove the rind. Place the Brie over the almond-jam mixture.

Bake for 7 minutes, until the Brie melts. Cut into squares and serve immediately.

RASPBERRY JAM

MAKES ABOUT 2 CUPS

3 cups ripe raspberries   **3 cups sugar**

In a nonreactive enameled or stainless steel pot, cook the raspberries over medium heat for 5 minutes, until mushy. Add the sugar and bring to a boil. Cook for 20 minutes at a boil, mashing the raspberries as they cook with a potato masher. When the raspberry mixture forms a gel and clings to a spoon, turn off the heat. If you have an instant read thermometer, boil the mixture to 220°F. Let cool.

THE

COCKTAIL

PARTY

"Cocktail" and "party" are two words that preps love, especially when served together. A cocktail party almost always occurs on a Saturday night (although hosting one on Friday won't hurt a bit). Some preps make every night a cocktail party, and that's just fine. It can be a relaxed gathering, but more often than not, it is a great excuse to put on a party dress or your favorite camel hair blazer and head out for the evening.

I find that the easiest cocktail parties to host are the ones where the bar is the centerpiece. A few choice hors d'oeuvres can serve as alcohol absorbers. But sometimes I like to go all out and serve showstopping food with wine and Champagne. Pick and choose as the occasion merits.

MENU FOR A
FORMAL COCKTAIL PARTY

A good preppy gets invited to lots of parties—and attends with glee. However, the obligation of returning the invitation can weigh heavily on the mind. The easiest way to be polite and return the favor of all those fun gatherings is to have a big cocktail party. It's a great way to show how loaded with friends and business associates you are while also fulfilling the social obligation.

Cheese platter

Store-bought crudités

Smoked Salmon Cucumber Rounds (page 175)

Lobster Salad on Endive Spears (page 172)

Chicken Liver Pâté (page 157) with crackers

Rosemary Shortbreads with Tomato Confit (page 151)

Filet Mignon on Baguette (page 163) with horseradish sauce

Quintessential Crab Dip (page 167)

Chicken Salad Cups (page 172)

Curried deviled eggs

Classic Shrimp Cocktail with Tequila-Lime Sauce (page 152)

Full bar

ROSEMARY SHORTBREADS
WITH TOMATO CONFIT

MAKES 12 DOZEN HORS D'OEUVRES

This sweet little canapé has a long, long history at Picnic. My assistant Jen, who was, at the time, a high school kid taking culinary classes, was given the job to create a ratio of butter to flour with just a hint of sweet that would hold up as an hors d'oeuvre. Well, she spent days, perhaps weeks, working on that ratio. When she finally had it done, and done perfectly, someone threw away her recipe! When she finally figured it out again, she wrote it in permanent marker on our wall. We looked at that wall, a lot. Jen made thousands of these little bites.

This savory shortbread is great for vegetarians, and because the tomatoes are made into a confit, this recipe can be made just about anytime of the year.

FOR THE SHORTBREAD ROUNDS
2 cups flour
¼ cup confectioners' sugar
¼ teaspoon salt
¼ teaspoon baking powder
1 cup butter, softened
2 tablespoons finely chopped fresh
   rosemary

FOR THE TOMATO CONFIT
2 cups diced fresh tomatoes
2 tablespoons olive oil
1 tablespoon butter
1 tablespoon balsamic vinegar
½ teaspoon salt
¼ teaspoon pepper
2 tablespoons finely shredded fresh basil

For the shortbreads: In a large bowl, sift together the flour, sugar, salt, and baking powder. Using a standing mixer fitted with the paddle attachment, beat the butter on high speed, until light in color. Reduce the mixer speed to medium and slowly add the flour mixture until incorporated. Add the rosemary and beat until combined. Wrap the dough in plastic wrap and refrigerate for 1 hour.

Preheat the oven to 350°F.

Roll out the dough until it's about ⅛ inch thick. Use a 1-inch cookie cutter or any other small fun shape to cut out rounds. Place on a baking sheet.

Bake for 12 to 14 minutes, until golden brown. Transfer to a wire rack to cool.

For the tomato confit: In a small heavy-bottomed saucepan, combine the tomatoes, oil, butter, vinegar, salt, and pepper. Cook over very low heat for about 45 minutes, until the tomatoes are completely broken down.

Stir in the basil and cook 5 minutes more. Taste and add salt and pepper as needed.

Serve warm, or refrigerate for up to 2 days in a sealed container.

To serve the hors d'oeuvres, arrange some shortbreads on a pretty platter. Top each with a little bit of confit.

CLASSIC SHRIMP COCKTAIL
WITH TEQUILA-LIME SAUCE

MAKES APPROXIMATELY 30 PIECES

For many, many years, shrimp cocktail was the start to any great restaurant meal. History takes it back to the early 1900s. Talk about a dish that has never gone out of favor! It was served, in preppy fashion, in special little shrimp cocktail cups that had two segments, one for crushed ice and one for the shrimp and cocktail sauce or mayonnaise.

I can't think of a single event I have catered where the shrimp cocktail platter was not the first thing to disappear. It's as classic as a patch pocket on a tweed jacket.

FOR THE SHRIMP
2 tablespoons Old Bay seasoning
1 tablespoon pickling spice
3 bay leaves
2 pounds colossal shrimp, peeled, deveined, and tail on
Ice for cooling

FOR THE SAUCE
1 cup ketchup
2 tablespoons prepared horseradish, or to taste
3 tablespoons tequila
Juice of 2 limes

For the shrimp: In a large pot, bring 6 quarts of water to a boil over high heat. Add the Old Bay, pickling spice, and bay leaves. Add all of the shrimp at once and let the water return to a boil. As soon as the water boils again, drain the shrimp in a colander and immediately cover with ice.

For the sauce: In a small bowl, combine the ketchup and horseradish. Stir in the tequila and lime juice. Refrigerate for up to 2 days in a sealed container.

Serve the shrimp on a platter with the sauce in a dipping cup.

Old-Fashioned

OLD-FASHIONED

There is a reason that this drink has been around for decades upon decades. Is it somewhat old-fashioned? Sure, but so what. That is exactly the way we like it.

1 sugar cube
Dash of club soda
2 dashes of Angostura bitters
2 jiggers of bourbon whiskey

1 cup cracked ice
1 ½-inch strip orange peel
2 maraschino cherries

Put the sugar cube in a chilled cocktail shaker and splash the club soda over it. Crush the sugar cube with a muddler. Swirl the shaker for 20 seconds, until the sugar fully dissolves. Add the bitters, whiskey, and ice, and shake. Strain into a chilled double old-fashioned glass.

Squeeze the orange peel over the cocktail, making sure the orange oil falls into the glass. Garnish with the maraschino cherries.

MOSCOW MULE

History tells us that vodka was not popular when it was first introduced here in the States. It seems that, like our preppy people, most preferred gin to the rather tasteless vodka. Then the Moscow Mule came along in the Thirties and a vodka craze was born. The nifty thing about the Moscow Mule is that it calls for ginger beer, which, of course, is already stocked in the preppy bar for the famous Dark and Stormy (page 90).

½ lime
2 fluid ounces vodka

4 fluid ounces ginger beer

Squeeze the lime juice into a collins glass or copper mug (if you're really being authentic). Drop the wedge into the glass. Add the vodka and ginger beer and stir. Add ice.

GENTLEMEN USE A CHURCH KEY

When opening a beer, a gentleman should use a church key; not some piece of scrap metal on his key chain, and certainly not his teeth. A church key is a tool that every bar used to have because there were no such thing as a screw cap or a pop-top for bottles or cans. A church key is typically a flat piece of pressed metal that often has two ends; one end opens bottles and the other pierces cans. You may know it simply as a "bottle opener."

Believe it or not, the twist-off bottle cap is a fairly recent invention. Beverage cans were once simply cans, just like canned soup, with a sealed top and bottom and no opening at all. I remember the brands of beer my father would serve; Rheingold, Schaefer, and Pabst come to mind. My dad would make two punctures: one to drink from and the second one was an airhole, so the beer would flow easily.

In fact, there are still many products, both at the bar and in the kitchen, that you won't be able to open without this implement. It is classic and classy to open your beverage with a church key. And gentlemen still should.

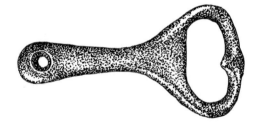

CHICKEN LIVER PÂTÉ

MAKES 2 CUPS

When I was a young whippersnapper, I chaired my first charity event. It was quite an honor to be asked to do that at the age of 24. The event was an outdoor cocktail party, and one of my tasks was to find a caterer. I was unhappy with the prices they were charging and came up with the brilliant (read: silly) idea that I could make the food myself with the help of a few friends. One of the things I wanted was a pâté, so I turned to the *Silver Palate Cookbook*, perhaps the most iconic cookbook of preppy's glory days. I've changed the recipe over the years, just a bit, and it is a great pâté. Thanks to that book, I pulled the party off, by the skin of my Lacoste shirt.

½ cup chopped onion
¼ cup vegetable oil
1 pound chicken livers, cleaned
1 cup butter, softened
Pinch of cayenne pepper
1 tablespoon dry mustard
1 teaspoon ground nutmeg
½ teaspoon ground allspice

½ teaspoon ground cloves
2 garlic cloves
¼ cup brandy
¼ cup heavy cream
2 teaspoons salt
1 teaspoon white pepper
¼ cup finely chopped dried figs

In a large sauté pan, sweat the onions in the oil about 5 minutes, until just translucent. Add the livers and sauté for about 7 minutes, until the livers are just slightly pink on the inside. Turn off the heat and drain off the fat.

In a food processor, combine the liver-onion mixture, butter, cayenne, mustard, nutmeg, allspice, cloves, and garlic, processing until smooth. Add the brandy, cream, salt, and white pepper and process about 2 minutes more, until silky smooth. Scrape into a bowl and stir in the figs.

Transfer to a four cup serving bowl and chill overnight. Refrigerate for at least 1 day and up to 2 days. Serve with crackers or crusty bread.

FONDUE!

SERVES 6

Back in the seventies, the biggest hit of the cocktail party circuit was a fondue setup. My aunt Krin lived in Switzerland for quite a while and used this recipe for her fondue parties. If you don't have a fondue set, well, you can wing it any way you like. A heavy pot over Sterno and long skewers work just fine.

I've written the recipe exactly as she did and, gee, is it tasty. It's a fun addition to a cocktail party or it can create a party unto itself. Serve with a few casseroles (pages 24–25) and you've got yourself a retro dinner party.

2 cups dry white wine
1⅓ pounds Emmentaler cheese, finely
   grated (about 3¼ cups)
1⅓ pounds mild cheddar cheese, finely
   grated (about 3¼ cups)
2 tablespoons cornstarch

3 tablespoons kirsch
¼ teaspoon ground nutmeg
¼ teaspoon paprika
¼ teaspoon baking soda
Baguette cubes for dipping

Pour the wine into the fondue pot or an enameled or other heavy-bottomed pot and heat over high heat until it starts to boil. Add the Emmentaler and cheddar cheeses, bit by bit, constantly stirring with a wooden spoon in a figure-eight pattern. Stir and cook over high heat until the cheese is melted and has a creamy consistency.

In a small bowl, stir together the cornstarch and kirsch until the cornstarch dissolves. Add the kirsch mixture to the cheese, followed by the nutmeg, paprika, and baking soda, constantly stirring.

Place the fondue pot over a burner in the center of the table. Serve with baguette cubes and fondue forks.

A CASUAL SATURDAY NIGHT GET-TOGETHER

This menu is perfect for a twentysomething casual cocktail party. The food is minimal. The budget goes to the beverages. The guests don't mind a bit.

Wheat Thins, store-bought Brie wedge covered with raspberry jam

Green grapes

Olives from the grocery store olive bar

Eileen's Crabbies (page 19)

Mini quesadillas

Bag of chips and jar of salsa, served from the bag and jar

Mixed nuts, served from the can

THE DIVIDEND

Don, a great sailor (think Bermuda Race entrant), has an expression he calls "the dividend." When you make a drink in a shaker, usually there is a bit left after you pour a full drink. He fondly refers to that as "the dividend," because when you finish your drink you get a little return, the half a drink or so in the shaker.

MINI CRANBERRY MEATBALLS

FEEDS A CROWD AS AN HORS D'OEUVRE

At a cocktail party, it is standard to have a number of stationary items that people can snack on while waiting for a tray of passed hors d'oeuvres to be brought to them. Mini meatballs of any type do the trick. They are quick, easy, and a casual contrast to the more formal food being served. Sometimes I serve Swedish meatballs, but this old campy favorite is the winner.

2 pounds ground beef, such as chuck
1 cup fresh white bread crumbs
2 eggs beaten
⅓ cup finely chopped fresh parsley
3 cloves garlic, minced
2 teaspoons onion powder
1 teaspoon seasoned salt

1 teaspoon celery salt
Pinch of cayenne pepper
1 14-ounce can whole-berry cranberry
 sauce
1¼ cups chili sauce, such as Heinz
2 tablespoons packed light brown sugar
Juice of 1 lemon

Preheat the oven to 325°F.

In a large bowl, combine the beef, bread crumbs, parsley, garlic, onion powder, seasoned salt, celery salt, and cayenne. With wet hands, form the beef mixture into 1-inch balls. Place the meatballs 1 inch apart on a baking sheet. Bake for 15 minutes, until lightly browned.

While the meatballs are baking, make the sauce. In a large saucepan, combine the cranberry sauce with the chili sauce over low heat for about 10 minutes, until the cranberry sauce is fully melted. Add the brown sugar and lemon juice and cook for 5 minutes, until the sugar has melted. Add the cooked meatballs to the sauce, gently spooning the sauce over them.

Continue cooking over low heat, stirring frequently, for 45 minutes, or transfer the meatballs and sauce to a Crock-Pot and cook for 1 hour on low heat. Serve from the Crock-Pot or transfer to a casserole dish. Have toothpicks handy for picking up the meatballs.

THE GARNISH MAKES THE DRINK

- Martinis are comprised of gin and a splash of vermouth. The olive is the garnish.
- Dirty martinis are a classic martini with olive juice and two additional olives.
- Gibsons are comprised of gin and a splash of vermouth. A cocktail onion is the garnish.

THE BOTTOM SHELF

It is almost impossible to believe, but Boone's Farm wines still exist. Made by Gallo, there are a few flavors available these days. I dared taste one, and it was no Country Kwencher, Tickle Pink, or Apple Ripple. Strawberry Hill, indeed, still exists. This cheap, low-quality, almost fruit punch–like wine was the illegally purchased first sip of wine by many a young prep. When our parents found out, they were appalled that we were drinking what was and is considered "ripple wine" always found on the bottom shelf of the wine racks at the store. Back in the day, it ran for about a buck. It was never drunk out of a glass, only from the bottle.

Over the years, as we grew, so did our taste buds, thank goodness. Here are some key types of wine to always keep on hand, ready to open at the slightest need or want.

WHITE
- Sancerre: Crisp, light, summery, and perfect for a spritzer.
- California Chardonnay: Big, buttery, and full of oak. Great with light meats and as a sipping wine.
- White Burgundy: Also made from the Chardonnay grape but with more finesse. I love a good Meursault.

RED
- Burgundy: The Pinot Noir grape is the major player in this red. Red Burgundies are far superior to American pinots. A beautiful Charmes-Chambertin will surely impress.
- Bordeaux: Some would say red Bordeaux is the jewel of French wines, although others will say Burgundy rules. I adore Cos d'Estournel.
- Old-vines Zinfandel: Pick a reasonably priced American Zin for holiday entertaining.
- California Cabernet: When the occasion doesn't warrant a Burgundy or Bordeaux.

FORTIFIED WINE
- Tawny Port: Vintage if possible.

FILET MIGNON on BAGUETTE

APPROXIMATELY 70 PIECES

A whole tenderloin gracing the table is a preppy staple. Slice it thinly, drench it in butter, and serve it on toast points or baguettes and it becomes a real treat. Make sure to cook the tenderloin to medium-rare or rare because it will cook more in the butter.

1 5- to 6-pound beef tenderloin, trimmed
    by the butcher
1 cup butter
3 tablespoons salt

2 tablespoons pepper
Baguette slices or toast points for
    serving

Preheat the oven to 450°F.

Place the tenderloin on a baking sheet or jelly roll pan and tuck the thin end of the meat under. Slather the tenderloin with ½ cup of the butter. Season with the salt and pepper.

Roast for 15 to 20 minutes, until an instant-read thermometer inserted in the thickest part of the roast measures 130°F (this is one of those times you really need a meat thermometer). Let rest, covered loosely in foil, for at least 30 minutes and up to 2 hours. Thinly slice the tenderloin.

In a small saucepan, melt the remaining ½ cup of butter over medium low heat, until it simmers; do not let it brown. Reduce the heat to low. Add the slices of tenderloin to the butter to rewarm and reach the desired level of doneness.

Serve on baguette slices or slices of white bread, crusts removed, and cut in half on the diagonal. Season with salt and pepper to taste.

DEVILED EGGS

FOR 24 PIECES

eviled eggs were perhaps the most popular appetizer at my restaurant. Whenever I am a guest at a picnic, I bring a few dozen, and they disappear faster than you can say Fourth of July. The trick, indeed, is in the boiling of the eggs.

12 extra-large or jumbo eggs
½ cup mayonnaise, or to taste
1 teaspoon dry mustard

½ teaspoon sweet or hot paprika (optional)

Place the eggs in a large pot and add enough cold water to cover by at least 1 inch. Bring just to a boil over high heat and turn off the heat immediately. Do not cover the pot. Let the eggs sit in hot water for 16 minutes.

Drain the eggs, and cover with ice and cold water. Let the eggs sit in the ice bath for 20 minutes.

Carefully peel the eggs under running water, or in the ice bath water. Cut the eggs in half lengthwise. Carefully remove the yolks and put them in a small bowl. Put the whites in a bowl of cold water.

Place the yolks in a food mill and sprinkle the mustard over them. Run the eggs through the mill into a medium bowl. If you don't have a food mill, go ahead and with a rubber spatula force the yolks through a fine sieve.

Gently fold the mayonnaise into the yolks. Place in a piping bag, if desired.

Remove the whites from the water and drain on a paper towel–lined plate.

Pipe or spoon the yolk mixture into the whites, mounding it slightly. Sprinkle with paprika, if desired.

Serve immediately.

TOPPINGS FOR DEVILED EGGS

White truffle salt

Snipped fresh chives

Fresh dill and caviar

Smoked paprika

Finely chopped cornichons

Finely chopped dry-cured olives

1 tablespoon Madras curry powder in egg yolk mixture

THE VODKA MATRIX

orange + VODKA = Screwdriver

cranberry + orange + VODKA = Madras

cranberry + pineapple + VODKA = Bay Breeze

grapefruit + VODKA = Greyhound

cranberry + grapefruit + VODKA = Seabreeze

cranberry + VODKA = Cape Codder

tomato + VODKA = Bloody Mary

QUINTESSENTIAL CRAB DIP

SERVES 12-14

Heavens, there are a lot of versions of hot crab dip. As a kid, I remember being allowed downstairs for the beginning of my parents' frequent dinner parties, and always seeing this dip on the coffee table, surrounded by crackers. I'd sneak a bite or two. When I was old enough to go to cocktail parties myself, I felt oh so grown-up bringing this dip along and telling the host to simply pop it in the oven for ten minutes. Heck, I still bring it to parties, and everybody gets a chuckle out of its old-school flavor and look.

2 8-ounce packages cream cheese, softened
2 tablespoons whole milk
1 16-ounce can backfin or special crabmeat
¼ cup finely chopped sweet onion

1 teaspoon creamy prepared horseradish
1 teaspoon salt
½ teaspoon white pepper
⅔ cup slivered almonds
Crackers, for serving

Preheat the oven to 350°F.

In a large bowl, combine the cream cheese and milk. In another large bowl, combine the crabmeat, onion, horseradish, salt, and pepper. Fold the crab mixture into the cream cheese mixture. Transfer to a 2-quart casserole dish, and sprinkle almonds on top.

Bake for 15 minutes, until nice and bubbly. Serve immediately with lots of crackers.

TUNA TARTARE ON CRISPY WONTONS

MAKES ABOUT 50 HORS D'OEUVRES

Timing is essential with these rather labor-intensive bites, but the end result is well worth the effort. Your guests will be pleased that you seemingly cared enough about them to go to this extreme.

1 quart vegetable oil
25 wonton wrappers, cut in half on the diagonal
1½ pounds sushi-quality tuna
3 tablespoons olive oil
3 tablespoons finely chopped fresh cilantro

2 teaspoons lime juice
2 teaspoons ground cumin
1 teaspoon salt
2 ripe mangoes
3 ripe Hass avocados

For the crisps: Have a paper towel-lined plate or wire rack over a baking sheet next to the stove.

In a large pot, heat the vegetable oil over high heat until it reaches 350°F. Working in small batches, carefully lower the wontons into the oil and fry for about 1 minute, until golden brown and crispy. With a slotted spoon, transfer to the paper towel–lined plate to drain. (The wonton crisps may be fried up to 4 hours in advance.)

For the tartare: Finely dice the tuna, being careful to remove any sinew. Transfer to a sealed container and refrigerate until just before serving. (The tuna may be diced up to 2 hours in advance.)

Make the dressing: In a large bowl, whisk together the olive oil, cilantro, lime juice, cumin, and salt. (The dressing may be prepared up to 1 day in advance.)

When the party starts: Cut the mangoes and the avocados into fine cubes. With your hands, gently combine the mangoes, avocados, and tuna. Add the dressing, and carefully toss with your hands.

Top each wonton crisp with the tuna mixture. Serve immediately.

Note: If you are serving this hors d'oeuvre in batches, add the dressing as you prepare each batch. If added earlier, the lime will begin to "cook" the tuna, turning it an unappealing brown color.

WHISKEY SOUR

SERVES 2

I think of a whiskey sour as one of those coming-of-age cocktails. It's sweet, it hides the taste of the whiskey, and it is rather strong. I remember drinking scotch sours that we shook with a powdered mix. This sour is nice and fresh, crisp, and harkens to those college days of yore.

FOR THE SIMPLE SYRUP
¼ **cup sugar**
½ **cup water**

FOR THE COCKTAIL
4 **fluid ounces Irish or Scotch Whiskey**
 (Jameson's works just dandy)

3 **ounces simple syrup**
2 **ounces fresh lime juice**
1 **ounce fresh lemon juice**
Ice cubes
Maraschino cherry for garnish

For the simple syrup: In a small saucepan over medium heat bring the water to a simmer. Add the sugar and whisk until fully incorporated. Cool. Reserve any unused syrup in the fridge for up to 1 week.

For the cocktail: Combine all the ingredients, except for the cherry, in a shaker with plenty of ice, and shake vigorously until frothy. Pour into a double old-fashioned glass and garnish with the cherry. Sip with love.

FAST AND EASY HORS D'OEUVRES

These hors d'oeuvres are simple, quick, and tasty. With a little garnish and a pretty platter, they are a perfect addition to a cocktail party. Remember: Double the booze and halve the food and your party will be a hit!

BLUE CHEESE AND WALNUT SPREAD ON ENDIVE SPEARS
Separate the endive leaves; no need to rinse them. Mix equal parts blue cheese and mayonnaise in a food processor. Squeeze in a bit of lemon juice. Transfer the spread to a piping bag or zip-top bag with one of the corners cut off. Pipe the spread into the endive leaves. Sprinkle with finely chopped walnuts.

LOBSTER SALAD ON ENDIVE SPEARS
Use the same method as above, using finely chopped lobster salad (page 43).

CHICKEN SALAD CUPS
Almost every grocery store now carries cute little phyllo cups in the frozen section. Pick either the Curried Chicken Salad (page 187) or the Harvest Chicken Salad (page 186), give it a pulse or two in a food processor, and fill the cups. Garnish each cup with a dried cranberry.

BRIE AND APRICOT BITES
Soak some dried apricots in warm water for a half hour. Pat dry. Bring Brie to room temperature and remove the rind. Scoop a small amount of Brie onto each apricot and top with a pecan half. Bake in a 350°F oven for 5 to 7 minutes, until the Brie melts slightly.

MINI TUNA MELTS

Spread a thin layer of tuna salad onto a slice of party rye bread. Top with a little shredded cheddar. Cut in half on the diagonal. Bake in a 350°F oven for about 3 minutes until the cheese melts.

REUBEN MELTS

Layer thin slices of corned beef and Swiss cheese and a dab of sauerkraut onto a slice of party pumpernickel bread. Spread Thousand Island dressing on another slice of bread and sandwich the two together. In a sauté pan with a little butter, lightly brown the sandwich over medium heat for about three minutes on each side or until the cheese melts. Cut in half on the diagonal.

QUICK AND EASY QUESADILLAS

Lay a flour tortilla or flour wrap (such as spinach, sun-dried tomato, whole wheat, or white) on a work surface. In a food processor, combine equal parts prepared salsa and cooked chicken. Thinly spread the chicken mixture on half of the tortilla. Add shredded cheddar or jack cheese, and fold the tortilla in half. In a large sauté pan, add 1 tablespoon of veggie oil and cook the tortilla about 3 minutes, until crispy on the bottom. Flip and cook the other side until crispy. Cut into 6 wedges and dollop each wedge with sour cream.

WILD MUSHROOM QUESADILLAS

Sauté fresh mushrooms in a little butter. Transfer the mushrooms to a food processor and add an equal part of goat cheese. Pulse and spread over the wraps as above.

SMOKED SALMON CUCUMBER ROUNDS

MAKES 30 CANAPÉS

Most hors d'oeuvres are truly easy to assemble. The trick is getting the timing right, so that it looks nice and fresh when your guests arrive. This canapé can be made about two hours in advance, then transferred to a serving platter. You can dress it up with caviar or make it more casual with capers. Either way, it is a lovely little bite.

1 English cucumber
2 ounces crème fraîche
Juice of 1 lemon
1 tablespoon finely chopped fresh dill

4 ounces smoked salmon, sliced into
   thin strips
30 capers or 1 small tin of osetra caviar
   (or American paddlefish if budget
   dictates)

Slice the cucumber into very thin rounds, about $\frac{1}{16}$ inch thick. Lay the rounds on a platter.

In a small bowl, combine the crème fraîche, lemon juice, and dill. Carefully place a small piece of salmon onto each cucumber round, and top with a small dollop of the crème fraîche mixture. Garnish with 1 caper or 1 small spoonful of caviar. Serve.

A RULE TO LIVE BY . . .

We preps do not believe in conspicuous consumption in general. However, cocktails and caviar are exceptions to this rule.

THE VEUVE CLICQUOT SITTING ROOM

Impress your friends with a Veuve Clicquot chair. This is a nifty little party trick that takes just a few minutes, with a bit of practice. You'll need a small needle-nose pliers.

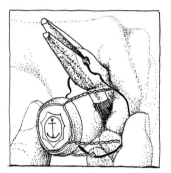 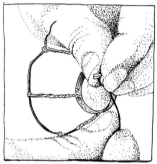 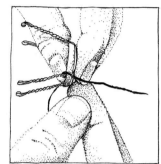

Completely untwist the bottom wire of the cage (the one you mostly untwisted to get the bottle open). Cut the wire in the center where you untwisted it, with the pliers, and carefully remove from the rest of the cage. Note, when it is gone, you have a little seat with four legs. Using the pliers, straighten the legs.

Bend the wire to form the back of the chair, and using the pliers, attach one end to one of the "legs." Repeat with one more leg.

At this point, you should have a plain chair. Now, using your pliers, work with the chair back.

Shape the chair back in as jolly a fashion as you like: a heart, a bistro chair, the possibilities are endless.

As you become more adept at the process, you can shorten the legs and make a stool, put two together for a settee. You can make a whole collection of your handiwork.

A NOTE ABOUT CHAMPAGNE

There are two Champagnes that are appropriate to pop at any preppy occasion, Veuve Clicquot and La Grande Dame Veuve Clicquot.

Cristal, not preppy. Dom Perignon, not preppy. California sparklers and prosecco, not preppy.

The label may be orange or, on a very special occasion, pink. That is all.

LUNCHEONS

AND

SHOWERS

ALL GROWN UP AND
GETTING MARRIED

Preps love to entertain. Baby coming? Someone getting married? All the more reason to get together. Let's face it, a good preppy would never have these events at a restaurant—why else have we amassed generations of sets of silver, china, and crystal?

CHILLED MIXED-BERRY RIESLING SOUP

SERVES 8 AS A FIRST COURSE

This refreshing summer soup serves two purposes. First off, it is a lovely and light first course for a luncheon or brunch. But the joy of this little starter is that the wine is added to the soup just before serving, allowing you to have an "adult" beverage without having to pour one! When choosing a Riesling, I recommend a German Trocken, the driest of the variety, or a nice French Riesling from Alsace. Do not use a late-harvest Riesling or you'll have a soup that can be served only for dessert.

1 pint fresh blueberries
½ pint fresh raspberries
2 pints fresh strawberries
1 cup cold water
Juice of 1 lemon
⅓ cup sugar

½ cup sour cream, plus more for garnish
1 cup light cream
1 teaspoon salt
1 cup Riesling wine, or to taste
Fresh mint leaves, for garnish

In a blender, puree the blueberries, raspberries, strawberries, water, and lemon juice on medium speed for 5 minutes, until completely pulverized.

Strain the berry mixture through a fine-mesh sieve placed over a large bowl. If you don't have a fine-mesh sieve, one layer of cheesecloth lining a colander will do. Use a ladle to push all the berries through the sieve. Scrape the bottom of the sieve with a rubber spatula to get all the fruit.

Transfer the strained berry mixture to a saucepan and add the sugar. Cook over medium heat and bring just to a simmer, until the sugar melts. Turn off the heat and let cool slightly.

Add the sour cream and whisk vigorously into the berries (well, not too vigorously, but use a little energy), until it is combined. Add the light cream and whisk vigorously again. Season with the salt.

Refrigerate for at least 1 hour and up to 4 hours.

Just before serving, stir in the wine.

Divide the soup among 8 bowls and garnish with a dollop of sour cream and 1 mint leaf.

A TYPICAL PREPPY SHOWER

Just like a luncheon, a shower is held at someone's home. (Never at the home of the mother of the bride/expectant mother.) The only possible exception is an afternoon tea at a fancy hotel. But that is the exception, not the rule. If it is a bridal shower, the more alcohol available the better for all involved. If it is a baby shower, out of politeness to the poor woman who has not been blotto in about seven months, well, iced tea, punch, and lemonade shows her that you feel her pain, even if a group of you go out immediately afterward for drinks.

A note on etiquette: It has become quite popular to forgo the hour or two of opening gifts in front of the guests. I applaud this new practice. First of all, do we really want to ooh and aah over food processors and breast pumps? Secondly, it gives guests more time to mix, mingle, and cocktail. Last of all, it stops the gift-giving madness of outdoing the Joneses. The guest of honor opens her gifts in private and then, of course, writes her handwritten thank-you notes.

A typical shower menu should start with some snacks or appetizers, because chances are, the guest of honor will feign surprise and arrive at least a half hour late. That's also a good time to start opening the wine and mixing the mimosas.

Here are a few ideas for a typical late-spring preppy shower.

FOR THE SNACKS
- Cheese platter with mild cheeses, green and red grapes, assorted crackers
- Veggie platter and store-bought dip
- Champagne Punch (page 198)

FOR THE LUNCHEON PORTION
- Platter of Tea Sandwiches (page 196)
- Poached Salmon Salad (page 190)
- New Potato Salad with Dill (page 45)
- Platter of Asparagus with Sauce Gribiche (page 193)
- Glazed Spiral Ham (page 201)
- Salad with Cucumbers, Blueberries, and Goat Cheese Vinaigrette (page 184)

FOR DESSERT
- Bakery cake

CHILLED ENGLISH PEA
AND MINT SOUP

SERVES 6 AS A FIRST COURSE

A nice chilled soup is a terrific way to start a formal luncheon. Fresh peas sing of spring. But if you cannot obtain fresh peas, go ahead and use frozen. However, really, the taste will change considerably.

2 cups fresh shelled peas
5 or 6 Boston lettuce leaves, torn into
    pieces
2 cups buttermilk

3 tablespoon chopped fresh mint leaves,
    plus whole leaves, for garnish
Salt and white pepper to taste
Crème fraîche, for garnish

Put the peas in a large pot and add enough water to cover. Bring to a boil over high heat, and cook about 4 minutes, until just tender. Drain the peas in a colander and cover with ice to cool quickly.

In a blender, puree the peas, lettuce, and buttermilk on high for 5 minutes, until well combined. Add the chopped mint and blend again. Taste and add salt and white pepper to taste.

Refrigerate for at least 1 hour and up to 12 hours.

Divide the soup among 6 bowls and top with crème fraîche and mint leaves.

SALAD with CUCUMBERS, BLUEBERRIES, AND GOAT CHEESE VINAIGRETTE

SERVES 6 AS A FIRST COURSE

When I had Picnic, my sous chef, Javier, was always trying to come up with new and different salads. The minute we put this on the menu, he knew he had a winner. It is refreshing and quite pretty to serve. Use, of course, the freshest of cucumbers you can find in season. During the rest of the year, choose English cucumbers (you know, the one that looks like it is wrapped in a condom).

FOR THE VINAIGRETTE
2 ounces fresh goat cheese, room temperature
4 tablespoons champagne vinegar
4 tablespoons vegetable oil
½ cup heavy cream
½ teaspoon salt
¼ teaspoon white pepper

FOR THE SALAD
10 cups assorted salad greens, such as butter lettuce, Bibb, baby arugula, and mâche, torn into bite-size pieces
2 cups cucumber, peeled and finely chopped
1 pint fresh blueberries

Chill 6 salad plates.

For the vinaigrette: In a blender, process the goat cheese, vinegar, oil, cream, salt, and white pepper on low speed, slowly increasing the speed to high until fully incorporated, about 2 minutes. Refrigerate for up to 1 week in a sealed container.

For the salad: In a large bowl, toss the greens with the vinaigrette. Use all of the vinaigrette or less, depending on how well dressed you like your salad.

Divide the dressed greens among 6 chilled salad plates. Top with the cucumber and blueberries. Serve immediately.

A TRIO OF CHICKEN SALADS

Perfect for a shower or luncheon, a trio of chicken salads offers a variety of flavors and textures and can be made the day before. I serve them with a nice tossed salad, a basket filled with breads, rolls, and croissants, and a platter of sliced tomatoes. Guests may choose to make a sandwich or put the chicken salads over greens.

A note about cooking the chicken for all three of the salads: You can simmer and cool your own chicken breasts. I like to poach them in salted water with a bit of white wine and a bay leaf. Bring the chicken to a boil, cover, and turn off the heat. Let the chicken poach in the liquid for about 25 minutes, until it registers 160°F on an instant-read thermometer. The resting chicken will reach 165°F.

But there is nothing wrong with zipping out to the grocery store and buying rotisserie chickens. I find that even though there is some dark meat, a roasted breast is moister and a bit more flavorful than a poached breast. Not only that, it shaves about a half an hour off your cooking time. For all of the recipes, double the mayonnaise mixture if using poached chicken. It absorbs much more of the mayo than the roasted does.

HARVEST CHICKEN SALAD

SERVES 6

At my first take-out lunch place, we wanted to do a pretty autumn chicken salad. The color is just lovely—dark pink. One of the local nonprofits actually based its logo on the color of this salad. We were quite pleased with that!

2 cups cooked chicken, shredded or cut into ¼-inch cubes

¾ cup canned whole berry cranberry sauce

¾ cup mayonnaise

1 Granny Smith apple, cut into ¼-inch cubes

½ cup minced red onion

½ cup walnut pieces

Put the chicken in a medium bowl. In a small bowl, combine the cranberry sauce and mayonnaise. Toss the chicken with the cranberry-mayonnaise mixture. Fold in apple and onion.

Refrigerate, covered, for 2 hours and up to 24 hours. Fold in the walnuts, and serve on a platter.

Note: If using roasted chicken, discard (or in my case, eat) the skin and shred all of the dark and white meat. I find that one small roasted chicken yields the 2 cups. If using poached chicken breasts, cut into ¼-inch cubes.

CHICKEN SALAD with PECANS and GRAPES

SERVES 6

A classic chicken salad, the addition of sherry vinegar and tarragon give it a nice little flavor punch. If you don't have fresh tarragon, dried will do just fine.

- 2 cups cooked chicken, shredded or cut into ¼-inch cubes)
- 1 cup mayonnaise
- 1 tablespoon sherry vinegar
- 1 tablespoon snipped fresh tarragon
- 1 teaspoon white pepper
- 1 cup green grapes, halved
- ½ cup toasted pecans

Put the chicken in a medium bowl. In a small bowl, combine the mayonnaise, vinegar, tarragon, and white pepper. Toss the chicken with the mayonnaise mixture. Fold in the grapes. Just before serving add the pecans.

Refrigerate, covered, for at least 2 hours and up to 24 hours. Serve on a platter.

CURRIED CHICKEN SALAD

SERVES 6

This chicken salad has a spicy and sweet component, with the flavors of Madras curry (which, by the way, is a British concoction) and dried fruits.

- 2 cups cooked chicken, shredded or cut into ¼-inch cubes
- ¾ cup mayonnaise
- ⅓ cup Major Grey's chutney
- 2 tablespoons Madras curry powder
- 1 teaspoon ground cumin
- ½ teaspoon turmeric (optional, see Note)
- ¼ cup dried apricots
- ½ cup dried currants
- ⅓ cup dry-roasted cashews

Put the chicken in a medium bowl. In a small bowl, combine the mayonnaise, chutney, curry powder, cumin, and turmeric. Toss the chicken with the mayonnaise-chutney mixture. Fold in the apricots, currants.

Refrigerate, covered, for at least 2 hours and up to 24 hours. Just before serving add the cashews.

Note: If you don't have turmeric, don't worry, it's only for color.

JAMMIN' HAM SANDWICHES

MAKES 12 SANDWICHES

The sweet and savory blend of these sandwiches are always a hit. Tasty and elegant, they are just swell on a buffet. At my lunch spot, I created this sandwich from a ham and brie grilled cheese sandwich. The elevated ingredients makes it worthy of a formal shower or luncheon.

12 fresh croissants
1½ pounds triple-crème cheese, such as
    Délice de Bourgogne, rind removed

1 12½-ounce jar best-quality raspberry
    jam or homemade jam (page 147)
1½ pounds sliced ham, such as jambon de
    Bayonne

Preheat the oven to 350°F.

Cut the croissants lengthwise, three quarters of the way through. Gently spread the cheese onto the cut bottom of each croissant, followed by the jam, dividing them evenly. Layer with 2 or 3 ham slices, depending on the ham's thickness. Cover with the croissant tops.

Place the sandwiches on a baking sheet and bake for 5 to 7 minutes, until the croissants are toasty.

Serve immediately.

POACHED SALMON SALAD

SERVES 6 AS A LUNCHEON ENTRÉE

ou will look like you worked really hard on this dish, when really you barely worked at all—which is always the better way!

1½ pounds salmon fillets
1 cup dry white wine
1 stalk celery
3 bay leaves
½ cup sour cream or crème fraîche
½ cup mayonnaise

3 tablespoons lemon juice
¼ cup chopped fresh dill
¼ cup chopped fresh parsley
¼ cup capers, rinsed
1 pound farfalle, cooked and cooled

Place the salmon in a large sauté pan with a tight-fitting lid. Add the wine and enough water to cover, plus the celery and bay leaves. Bring the liquid to a gentle simmer over medium low heat. The liquid should be barely moving. Cover and cook for about 15 minutes, depending on thickness, until the salmon lightly flakes with a fork but is still somewhat translucent in the center. Transfer to a platter and let cool for 10 minutes.

While the salmon cooks, in a small bowl, combine the sour cream, mayonnaise, and lemon juice. Stir in the dill, parsley, and capers.

Flake the salmon into a large bowl, add the pasta, and fold. Gently toss the salmon and pasta with the sour cream mixture.

Serve immediately or refrigerate, covered, up to 24 hours. I like to serve the salmon salad over a torn green salad.

MAYONNAISE, THE PREPPIEST OF CONDIMENTS

A nice deli has its mustard. A good burger joint has plenty of ketchup, hopefully Heinz. And a great hot dog place has its chili. Well, we preps put mayonnaise on just about anything. It is the condiment that pulls together many a recipe and many a sandwich. What would a tuna sandwich be without mayonnaise? Green bean casserole would be lackluster. Lobster salad or shrimp salad would be nonexistent. Potato salad, mac salad, and coleslaw would be an entirely different dish.

We preps dip our French fries in mayo so that we feel very, well, French. We spread it on a liverwurst sandwich, along with mustard. We are counted on to bring a covered dish that has mayonnaise as an ingredient.

Here are just a few nice ways to dress up the preppy condiment of choice:

- **Cranberry mayonnaise (great on a turkey sandwich):** 2 parts mayo, 1 part canned whole berry cranberry sauce

- **Dijon mayonnaise (terrific with ham):** 2 parts mayo, 1 part Dijon mustard

- **Chipotle mayonnaise (when you are feeling sophisticated):** 1 cup mayo, 2 tablespoons chipotle powder, 1 tablespoon hot paprika

- **Barbecue mayonnaise (summer all year):**
  1 cup mayo, ¼ cup barbecue sauce

- **Curried mayonnaise (perfect for tea sandwiches):**
  1 cup mayo, 2 tablespoons Madras curry powder,
  1 tablespoon ground cumin, 1 teaspoon turmeric

ASPARAGUS WITH SAUCE GRIBICHE

SERVES 6 AS A SIDE DISH

Asparagus is such a cheery vegetable. While it is available year-round, there is nothing like the tender local spears that arrive in spring. A friend of mine has an asparagus patch and the taste of just-picked asparagus is incomparable. If you can find it at a local farm, it is truly far superior to the spears standing straight up in water and bunched together with a rubber band at the supermarket.

Chilled blanched asparagus is a lovely way to serve them. The sauce gribiche is a variation on tartar sauce. Purists would make their own mayonnaise, but I think Hellmann's works just dandy.

Technically, asparagus is the one vegetable that should be picked up and eaten with your fingers. However, when slathered in sauce such as gribiche or hollandaise, a fork is acceptable. If the sauce is served on the side, feel free to pick up your spears and dip them right in.

3 hard-cooked eggs
½ cup mayonnaise
2 tablespoons Dijon mustard
1 tablespoon white wine vinegar
2 tablespoons capers
3 cornichons, finely chopped
2 tablespoons finely chopped fresh chervil

2 tablespoons finely chopped fresh tarragon
2 tablespoons finely chopped fresh parsley
36 thin asparagus spears, trimmed and lightly peeled at the base

Remove the yolks and finely chop the egg whites. Press the yolks through a fine-mesh sieve or food mill.

In a large bowl, combine the eggs and mayonnaise. Stir in the mustard and vinegar, followed by in the capers and cornichons. Slowly stir in the chervil, tarragon, and parsley. Refrigerate for up to 2 days in a sealed container.

Have a large bowl of ice water ready that is big enough to fit the asparagus spears next to the stove.

In a large pot, bring heavily salted water to a boil over high heat. When the water is vigorously boiling, add the asparagus and cook about 3 minutes, until just tender. Immediately plunge the asparagus into a large bowl of ice water. Let cool.

When completely cooled, remove the asparagus and pat dry with paper towels. Wrap in dry paper towels and refrigerate for up to 2 hours.

To serve, arrange the asparagus on a platter and spoon some sauce over the top, serving the remaining sauce on the side.

SEARED TUNA NICOISE SALAD

SERVES 10-12

On a buffet, this salad is a real showstopper. It is colorful and fun, with components that offer something for everyone to enjoy. Serve some extra greens and a bowl of dressing on the side. Depending on how many items you are serving on the buffet, this can serve up to a dozen.

3 cups small new potatoes, quartered
¼ cup olive oil
1½ teaspoons salt
1½ teaspoons pepper
1½ pounds sushi-quality tuna, cut into 2-inch steaks
¼ cup vegetable oil
4 heads butter lettuce or other salad greens, torn into bite-size pieces
30 to 40 haricots verts, trimmed and blanched

6 hard-cooked eggs (see hard-cooked eggs for deviling on page 164)
2 6-ounce tins anchovy fillets, rinsed and patted dry
2 cups grape tomatoes, halved
1½ cups pitted Nicoise olives or other pitted olives
3 tablespoons capers, rinsed
Olive Vinaigrette (recipe follows)

Preheat the oven to 400°F.

In a bowl, toss the potatoes with the olive oil, ½ teaspoon of the salt, and ½ teaspoon of the pepper. Roast, stirring frequently, for 15 to 20 minutes, until the potatoes are nicely browned.

Season the tuna steaks with salt and pepper. In a large sauté pan, heat the vegetable oil over high heat. When it is good and hot, add the tuna steaks and sear for 1 minute on each side, so that the tuna is still very, very rare. Transfer the tuna to a plate and let cool. Cut the tuna into ¼-inch strips.

On a large platter, arrange the lettuce. On top of the greens, arrange the tuna, haricots verts, potatoes, eggs, anchovies, tomatoes, and olives. Sprinkle the capers over the top. Drizzle with Olive Vinaigrette, serving the remaining vinaigrette on the side.

OLIVE VINAIGRETTE

MAKES ABOUT 1 CUP

¼ cup pitted kalamata olives
3 tablespoons minced shallot
1 tablespoon Dijon mustard
2 tablespoons cider vinegar

½ cup vegetable oil
Juice of ½ lemon
1 teaspoon white pepper
Salt to taste

In a blender, process the olives, shallot, mustard, vinegar, oil, lemon juice, and white pepper on low speed for about 2 minutes, until fully combined. Taste and add salt to taste. (It may not need salt, depending on how salty your olives are.) Refrigerate for up to 1 week in a sealed container.

TEA SANDWICHES, A PUNISHMENT
WITH GREAT REWARDS

Making perfect tea sandwiches are simply a royal pain in the neck. However, they are a must at a luncheon or tea party. When I am hosting a party that has tea sandwiches, well, I have a little party for a few friends the afternoon before. Many hands make light work, as the expression goes. Be sure to wrap the tea sandwiches in a slightly dampened paper towel and then tightly in plastic wrap. Refrigerate overnight.

Below are some filling ideas for classic tea sandwiches. With a little practice and imagination, you'll find there are many varieties that suit the tea sandwich. Think of your favorite combinations and simply make miniature versions. Open-faced, closed-faced, on little biscuits, the possibilities are as endless as the patience required to make them.

FILLINGS / CREAM CHEESE BASED

- **Cream cheese and maraschino cherry:** I believe this filling must have been created by someone who couldn't figure out what to fill a sandwich with! Perhaps they went to the bar looking for olives and only found maraschino cherries. The world will never know, but the fact is, it is a yummy little sandwich and adds a nice pink color to the platter of otherwise common-colored sandwiches.

  To make the filling: Soften an 8-ounce package of cream cheese and transfer to a large bowl. In a food processor, pulse ¼ cup of maraschino cherries with its juices until the cherries are just broken up a bit. Fold the cherries into the cream cheese.

- **Cream cheese and olive:** Use the same ratio and method as above.

- **Cream cheese and strawberry:** Soften cream cheese, spread on bread slices, and top with sliced fresh strawberries.

- **Cream cheese and chive:** Soften cream cheese and sprinkle with salt and pepper. Fold in snipped fresh chives. Use as filling along with smoked salmon or thinly sliced cucumber.

- **Cream cheese and raspberry jam:** Soften cream cheese and fold in ¼ cup seedless raspberry jam.

STANDARD FILLINGS

- **Tuna salad**

- **Egg salad**

- **Ham and Swiss with honey mustard**

- **Turkey and Havarti with cranberry mayo**

- **Ham salad:** Ask your local deli counter person to slice a piece of boiled ham ¾ inch thick. In a food processor, pulse until very finely chopped. Transfer to a bowl and fold in ⅓ cup mayo and ¼ cup sweet pickle relish.

- **Watercress and butter**

- **Thinly sliced radishes with butter and salt**

METHODS

- Tea sandwiches can be open-faced, closed, or cut with cookie cutters into fun little shapes, but they must never have crusts. Usually, they are usually cut into quarters.

- Do not overfill tea sandwiches. They are small, dainty bites. To add a nice touch, coat the sides of the sandwiches with a bit of mayo and then roll them in fresh herbs.

WHY NO CRUSTS?

- Some people eat crusts. Some do not. When serving a dainty bite like a tea sandwich, we need to accommodate our guests. Those that like crusts can live without them. Those that dislike them, well, they don't have to suffer, or worse, eat around the crust in front of others.

CHAMPAGNE PUNCH

SERVES 12

Punch is a dignified beverage, at least most of the time. Granted I can think back to many a spiked punch bowl at many a party, but as an adult, punch is genteel. For a shower, it is worth it to make a trip to the attic and dust off the punch bowl and glasses. Really, what other time would you use a punch bowl?

1 cup fresh raspberries
2 cups fresh blueberries
1 cup fresh blackberries
Juice of 2 lemons
½ cup simple syrup

2 bottles decent sparkling wine (an exception to drinking only Veuve, see page 176), such as Gruet
Ice Ring (recipe follows), for garnish

In a large punch bowl, stir together the raspberries, blueberries, blackberries, lemon juice, simple syrup, and sparkling wine. Garnish with the ice ring.

ICE RING

Fill a Jell-O mold or Bundt pan half way to the top with water. Add an assortment of berries, stone fruits, or edible flowers. When the mold is frozen, in about four hours, add additional water to the top of the pan. Freeze for 24 hours.

To unmold, place the frozen ice mold in boiling water for 10 seconds. Place in the punch.

WEDDING TIPS

I'm no Martha Stewart, but I have certainly catered my fair share of weddings over the years. Preppy weddings tend to be a bit low key. They are usually held outdoors, at the summer home of the bride's parents, with a lovely, tastefully decorated tent. The big day usually starts with the ceremony in the afternoon, followed by a cocktail reception. The older guests eventually leave, and the younger ones then have a late dinner.

If the parents do not have a summer home, the event occurs in the backyard of their house. If it is not summer, it is held at The Club.

Preps do not have destination weddings, unless they can afford to pay for each and every guest's trip and expenses.

Weddings are also not held at "wedding factory" types of catering halls or hotels. If the venue is to be a Veterans of Foreign Wars hall or similar, it's best that the couple elope.

GLAZED SPIRAL HAM

SERVES A CROWD

I can't think of a more strikingly festive centerpiece on a buffet table than a beautifully garnished glazed spiral-cut ham. It is perfect to serve at any time of year, for a large shower, a holiday buffet, an Easter brunch—really, whenever you want to feed a crowd. If you are lucky enough to have a local butcher that smokes its own spiral ham, you are really in business. If not, I love the unique corncob taste of the hams from the mail-order company Harrington's of Vermont. It is at least double the price of a supermarket ham, but for a splurge it is well worth it. Regardless of the brand you choose, make sure you get a fully cooked bone-in ham. The bone keeps it moist and flavorful.

1 13- to 15-pound bone-in spiral-cut ham
1½ cups water
1 cup maple syrup
1 cup packed light brown sugar
5 tablespoons Dijon mustard

1 teaspoon ground allspice
1 teaspoon ground cinnamon
1 teaspoon ground cloves
1 bunch grapes, for garnish

Preheat the oven to 300°F.

Place the ham in a large roasting pan. Pour the water, carefully around the ham, into the pan. Cover tightly with foil.

Bake for 2 hours.

After 1¾ hours, make the glaze. In a small saucepan, whisk together the maple syrup, brown sugar, mustard, allspice, cinnamon, and cloves. Bring to a simmer over low heat for about 2 minutes, until the glaze thickens. Turn off the heat.

When the ham is nice, warm, and juicy, remove the foil. Brush the glaze on the ham, reserving any remaining glaze for serving.

Raise the heat to 375°F and bake for 15 minutes more, until the glaze begins to bubble. If the ham seems cooked, add a little water to the bottom of the pan.

Transfer ham to a large platter and let rest 30 minutes. Remove half of the slices from the top bone end of the ham and arrange on the platter around the ham. Garnish the bone with a bunch of grapes, if you like, scattering others on the platter. Serve with the glaze on the side.

SCONES

12 SCONES

My friend Sally is very particular about tea and scones. Scones, according to proper British tradition, should never be served until afternoon teatime, usually around 4 o'clock in the afternoon. I thought she was going to have an absolute fit when she saw scones on the table at a luncheon I was hosting. Needless to say, she removed them from the table. Here is her recipe for scones.

2 cups flour
1 tablespoon baking powder
½ teaspoon salt
5 tablespoons butter, cut into small pieces

¼ cup shortening, cut into small pieces
⅓ cup whole milk
1 egg, beaten

Adjust the oven rack to the upper middle of the oven. Place a baking sheet in the oven and preheat the oven to 450°F.

In a large bowl, sift together the flour, baking powder, and salt. Sift again.

Using two knives or a pastry blender, cut the butter and shortening into the flour mixture until the mixture resembles soft bread crumbs.

Make a well in the center of the flour mixture and pour in the milk. Using a fork, gently draw the flour mixture into the center and stir it together with the milk. Draw in more of the flour mixture and continue stirring, until a soft dough forms.

Turn onto floured surface and knead 30 seconds, until a loose, smooth dough forms.

Roll out the dough until it's ¾ inch thick. Use a 2-inch cookie cutter to cut out rounds (do not twist the cookie cutter), or cut into triangles with a sharp knife.

With a spatula, transfer the scones onto the hot baking sheet, placing them 1 inch apart. Brush the tops with milk or egg.

Bake the scones 10 minutes, until golden brown. Transfer to a wire rack to cool.

Eat soon or freeze in an airtight container.

Variation: Sift ¼ teaspoon mixed spices (nutmeg, cinnamon, clove, allspice, and/or mace) into the flour mixture. Add 1 cup golden raisins or raisin-currant mix before adding the liquids.

APRICOT BARS

MAKES 24 BARS

y dear cousin Nan makes the best apricot bars. They are a perfect sweet ending to a luncheon. Many years ago, my mom was so impressed with them that she added them to her cookie repertoire.

1 cup flour
¼ teaspoon baking powder
½ teaspoon salt
4 tablespoons butter, melted
1 cup granulated sugar
2 eggs, beaten

1 cup dried apricots, finely chopped
    and soaked in hot water until soft
    (about 10 minutes), then drained
1 cup chopped pecans
Juice of 1 lemon
1 cup confectioners' sugar

Preheat the oven to 350°F. Line a buttered 9 x 13-inch baking pan with parchment paper. Butter the top of the parchment paper as well.

Using a standing mixer fitted with the paddle attachment, combine the flour, baking powder, and salt, then the melted butter, sugar, and eggs. Stir in the apricots and the pecans.

Spread the batter evenly in the prepared pan.

Bake for 25 minutes. Let cool in the pan for 15 minutes. Invert onto a wire rack and peel off the paper.

For the icing: Using a mixer with the paddle attachment, beat the lemon with the confectioners' sugar on high speed until fluffy.

Spread the icing on the apricot mixture and cut into 24 bars.

SALLY'S NOTE ABOUT TEA

Standard tea is tea with scones and jam—just a quick bite to curb the appetite until dinner. Afternoon tea is just that, a little nibble to tide you over served in the afternoon. It includes dainty tea sandwiches, scones, and a trifle or cookies.

High tea can stand in for supper and was more of a "working class" meal. It includes all the above with the addition of potted meats or meat pies. It was called high tea, because instead of the parlor chairs and gracious event that is afternoon tea, the chairs were high-backed and wooden. Others say it is named high tea because the table that tea was served on was high, whereas at an afternoon tea, the table was low. Either way, high tea is not highbrow. Afternoon tea is.

HOME

FOR THE

HOLIDAYS

Preps just love the holidays for too many reasons to count. Since our first Thanksgiving home from prep school—when we had an impromptu gathering with our hometown friends—we have embraced the holiday spirit.

The season is just one big party; from Thanksgiving to Christmas, we have an excuse to wear plaid and velvet, perpetually holding a cocktail in one hand. By New Year's Eve, the lucky preps are long gone, wearing madras again on a Caribbean island; those not so lucky tend to keep it low key. After all, we are starting the annual New Year's cleanse of swearing we will cut down on the G and Ts before five.

PEAR AND PARSNIP SOUP

SERVES 8

Pears and parsnips go together, well, like pears and parsnips! This simple, quick soup has a holiday flavor to it. The color however is a blandish white, so garnish it with some dried cranberries for a festive look.

½ sweet onion, minced
2 tablespoons butter
1 quart chicken stock
4 cups chopped peeled parsnips
1 pint heavy cream

2 ripe pears, such as Anjou, cut into
  chunks
Salt and pepper to taste
Dried cranberries for garnish

In a large stockpot over medium heat, sweat the onion in the butter for about 5 minutes. Add the stock and parsnips and cook for about 45 minutes, until the parsnips are soft. Check occasionally for stock level, adding water if the parsnips are not fully covered.

Working in batches, puree the parsnip mixture, heavy cream, and pears in the blender on medium speed about 5 minutes, until smooth. Add water if the soup is too thick. Season with salt and pepper. After pureeing and adding the cream, the soup will need to be re-warmed on low heat in a pot. Serve with a dried cranberry or two for garnish.

SWEET POTATO SOUP WITH MAPLE CREAM

SERVES 10-12

When I had my little gourmet shop, Thanksgiving was our dreaded day of cooking nonstop from Wednesday morning right through to the last pickup or delivery at 4 p.m. on Thursday. Our biggest seller: this tasty and colorful soup. I like to garnish it with little cubes of apple.

½ large sweet onion, chopped
1 tablespoon butter
1½ quarts chicken stock
4 cups sweet potato, peeled and cubed
1 tablespoon ground cinnamon
1 tablespoon ground nutmeg

1 quart heavy cream
2 tablespoons maple syrup, preferably Grade B
Salt and pepper to taste
Apple, for garnish

In a large stockpot over medium heat, sweat the onion in the butter for about 5 minutes. Add the stock, sweet potato, cinnamon, and nutmeg. Cook for about 1 hour, until the sweet potatoes literally fall apart.

Working in batches, puree the sweet potato mixture in a blender on medium speed about 5 minutes, until smooth. Add the cream and maple syrup, and puree about 2 minutes, until just combined. If the soup is too thick, add a bit of water.

Season with salt and pepper to taste.

To serve, rewarm the soup over low heat.

SWEET POTATO GRATIN

SERVES 8

While all families have their own sweet potato recipes (a good prep does not have one that includes mini marshmallows atop), I think this one is a great addition to the holiday table. It is a bit time-consuming, so I tend to assemble it in advance and then pop it into the oven in the morning. When dinner is almost ready, I put it back into the oven for about 15 minutes, then add the cheese for the final moments. Let it rest about 20 minutes, covered in foil, before serving. Sometimes I skip the cheese, making it more of a scalloped sweet potato.

1 quart heavy cream
⅓ cup maple syrup
4 large sweet potatoes, peeled and
   thinly sliced
1 cup butter, cut into pats

3 tablespoons flour
Salt to taste
2 cups grated mild cheddar cheese
   (optional)

Preheat the oven to 350°F. Butter a large casserole pan.

Warm the heavy cream and maple syrup in a heavy-bottomed saucepan over low heat for 5 minutes, whisking until combined.

Place a layer of the sweet potatoes in the pan. Dot them with pats of butter, a splash of the heavy cream–maple syrup mixture, and a light sprinkle of flour. Use your discretion on the quantities. Press down and continue to layer the sweet potatoes, butter, cream mixture, and flour until the pan is almost full. Season with salt every few layers. Pour the remaining cream mixture over the top, until the sweet potatoes are covered.

Bake for 90 minutes, until the cream has reduced and thickened and the potatoes are soft when pierced with a knife. If desired, sprinkle the cheese over the top and bake for a few minutes more, until the cheese has melted and browned.

Let stand for about 20 minutes, then cut into squares and serve.

CRANBERRY-ORANGE RELISH

ABOUT 3 CUPS

My father was one of seven kids, all of whom, as adults, gathered one day a year as a family: Thanksgiving. That meant six sisters and one brother, each with his or her spouse; their fifteen children, who also brought along spouses, dates, and eventually their children. It was quite a crowd, with almost fifty people.

Our family's Thanksgiving was very Norman Rockwell in many ways. With so many people, all of the furniture was cleared out of the living room so an extra table could be set. (And yes, because the house was so full, the youngest got stuck eating in the kitchen.) The cousins all played outside, waiting for dinner, and the sisters—six of them plus one in-law or outlaw—cooked, determined to make sure there was plenty of food (and if I recall, equally determined to outdo each other with the best side dish, turkey, stuffing, or dessert).

The buffet tables were laden with everything you could imagine. To this day, we cousins talk about those good old days, when it took three trips to the buffet table to sample all of the dishes. Dessert, well, that was a party unto itself.

This Cranberry-Orange Relish was always on the table. The cranberries are raw, which is a nice change from the cooked variety. All of my aunts had versions of this in their recipe boxes, so I really cannot give credit to any one of them. This is a family recipe indeed.

2 oranges
1 pound fresh cranberries

2 cups sugar

With a paring knife, carefully cut the rind off the oranges, following the curve of the fruit, leaving the bitter pith behind. Remove the seeds.

Press the cranberries, orange rind, and oranges through a meat grinder or process with the shredding blade of a food processor.

Transfer to a large bowl, and stir in the sugar. Refrigerate for 1 day, to allow the flavors to develop. Serve cold.

BRINING ᴀ TURKEY

G osh, people seem to make a huge to-do about the roasting of a turkey. It really is not that difficult. I do a couple of things to make it easier. First of all, I purchase some wing tips and legs and roast them the day before to make the gravy. That way, I only have to reheat the gravy on the big day.

The other thing I do is make a nice little brine. It is tough to fit a brining turkey in the fridge, so, personally, I only brine my turkey when the weather is good and cold and I can set it out on the screened porch, with ice, to keep the proper temperature, which must be between 33°F and 41°F.

1 turkey
1 gallon apple cider
1 cup packed light brown sugar

1 cup kosher salt
Ice, for the cooler

Place a large heavy-duty garbage bag in a big cooler and place the turkey in the bag (just remember to wash the cooler out before the first party of spring, when you will need it for beer). Pour the cider, sugar, and salt into the bag. With your hands, squish the salt and sugar around for a few minutes, until everything is mixed up well. Add enough water to cover the turkey.

Tie the top of the bag into a knot, and add enough ice to surround the bag in the cooler. Let the turkey brine for 2 days. Check the ice every so often, at least when it crosses your mind, to make sure it hasn't melted too much and to add more as needed.

After 2 days, transfer the bag with the turkey to your kitchen sink. Poke holes in the bag so that the brine drains. Remove the turkey and place it on a rack in a roasting pan. Let it rest at room temperature for about 1 hour. There will be a significant amount of liquid that drains from the turkey. Discard it, then roast the turkey any way your mama taught you!

Note: Make the gravy with the extra wing tips and legs, since the drippings from the brine will burn black on the bottom. Use your grandma's recipe. Some like their gravy with giblets, some like it smooth. Who am I to say?

LEFTOVER TURKEY SANDWICH

SERVES 1

It was my first time. The pounding headache, the wave of nausea: a hangover. The minute I felt it, I called my dear friend Mariann (who coincidentally gave me the recipe for Hangover Hash Browns, page 137). She told me to head to the nearest deli and order a turkey sandwich on white bread with a little mayo, lettuce, and tomato. I told her she was nuts. She promised me she was sane, so I dragged my green-faced body out of bed and bought the sandwich. Two hours later, I was as good as new.

I've eaten lots of turkey sandwiches on white bread over the years. The day after Thanksgiving is one I adore not just for the cure of that must-drink Nouveau Beaujolais, but also because it's a delicious sandwich.

2 slices white bread, such as Pepperidge Farm Brick Oven White

2 tablespoons Cranberry-Orange Relish (page 212)

¼ cup leftover stuffing

3 ounces turkey breast, thinly sliced

1 tablespoon mayonnaise

On 1 bread slice, spread the relish, followed by the stuffing and turkey. Spread the second bread slice with the mayonnaise. Assemble the sandwich and slice on the diagonal. Serve.

TURKEY TETRAZZINI

SERVES 4-6

I had forgotten all about tetrazzini until I was perusing an old Junior League cookbook, from the Junior League of Northern Virginia. The name of the book is *What Can I Bring?* and there, in the "Elegant Entrées" chapter, was a recipe for chicken tetrazzini. Long after we were all tired of turkey sandwiches, this was always the way my mom used up leftover Thanksgiving turkey. I made a few adjustments and, let me tell you, it is indeed a great way to use up that last bit of the turkey. Make it at the same time you are simmering up the turkey carcass for turkey soup, and use some of the stock in the recipe.

¼ cup butter
¼ cup flour
1 cup turkey stock or chicken stock
1 cup heavy cream
3 tablespoons sherry
Salt and pepper to taste
2 cups shredded cooked turkey

1 cup sliced button mushrooms
3 cups cooked spaghetti, vermicelli, or
  fettuccine
½ cup seasoned bread crumbs
¼ cup Romano, Gruyére, or Parmesan
  cheese

Preheat the oven to 350°F.

In a large saucepan, melt the butter over medium heat. Add the flour and cook, whisking constantly, for 2 minutes. Whisk in the turkey stock, followed by the cream, sherry, and salt and pepper. Bring to a boil over high heat. Reduce the heat to medium-low and simmer, stirring frequently, for 20 minutes, until there is no taste of flour. Turn off the heat.

In a 9 x 13-inch baking dish, combine the turkey, mushrooms, and pasta. Fold in the sauce. Bake for 25 to 30 minutes, until bubbly.

In a small bowl, combine the bread crumbs and cheese. Sprinkle evenly on top.

Bake 5 minutes more.

Let rest for 10 minutes and cut into squares. Serve from the baking dish.

TOMATO JELL-O MOLD

SERVES 8

1 3-ounce package lemon Jell-O
1 cup boiling water
1 cup condensed tomato soup
½ cup toasted pine nuts

20 pitted kalamata olives, sliced
½ cup finely diced celery
Lettuce leaves, for garnish
Mayonnaise, for garnish

Put the Jell-O in a heatproof bowl, add the boiling water, and stir until the Jell-O dissolves. Stir in the tomato soup and set aside to cool.

Lightly butter a 4-cup Jell-O mold. When the Jell-O mixture starts to thicken up a bit, stir in the pine nuts, olives, and celery. Pour into the mold and refrigerate for at least 4 hours and up to 24 hours.

Place the lettuce on a platter. Invert the mold, so that the Jell-O is turned onto the lettuce. Garnish with mayonnaise.

ODE TO A JELL-O MOLD

Oh jiggly, colorful, frightening thing
It's amazing how you stay in that ring!
Cabbages, nuts, mayo, and ham
Canned fruit, sour cream, and even some jam.
For a century you have graced the holiday spread
Filling all of our guests' heads with great dread
I can't help myself, there is nothing I can do
But to share every holiday table, with you!

ROASTED PORK LOIN WITH CUMBERLAND SAUCE

SERVES 6

Cumberland sauce is one of those spiffy little relish/chutney/pickled types of condiments that the Brits just love and, frankly, excel at.

Pork is the easiest roast to stick in the oven. If you buy a nice size roast and ask the butcher to not trim the fat, you will have a moist, succulent piece of meat without a problem. It is even better brined.

I've shared two recipes here, one brined, in which case, you must cook the vegetables separately. If you skip the brine, the vegetables will impart their own flavor to the pork.

3 cups apple cider
½ cup salt

¼ cup sugar
1 4-pound pork loin

In a small saucepan, bring the cider to a boil over high heat. Add the salt and sugar, and cook, stirring constantly, until they dissolve. Turn of the heat and let cool completely.

Place the pork in a large nonreactive bowl or deep roasting pan making sure the sides of the bowl are at least 1 inch higher than the pork. Pour the cider mixture over the pork and add enough water to cover the pork.

Refrigerate for 1 to 2 days.

Remove the pork from the brine 1 hour before cooking and pat dry with paper towels. Preheat the oven to 350°F. Place a roasting rack in a roasting pan.

Place the pork, fat side up, on the rack. Roast until the pork registers 140°F on an instant-read thermometer, about 45 minutes. Transfer the pork to a platter, cover loosely with foil, and let rest 25 minutes.

Carve into thin slices and serve on a platter.

CUMBERLAND SAUCE

MAKES ABOUT ¾ CUP

1 lemon, peeled
1 orange, peeled
½ cup red currant jelly

¼ cup port
1½ teaspoons dry mustard
1½ teaspoons ground ginger

Thinly slice the lemon and orange rind. Bring a small saucepan halfway filled with water to a boil over high heat. Add the lemon and orange rinds and boil for 5 minutes to remove any bitterness. Transfer to a small bowl and set aside.

In another small saucepan, combine the jelly and port over low heat and cook about 5 minutes, whisking frequently, until combined. Strain through a fine-mesh sieve over a small bowl.

In a small serving bowl, mix the mustard, ginger, juice of ½ lemon and juice of 1 orange. Stir in the jelly-port mixture. Add the lemon and orange rinds and stir again.

Refrigerate for at least 1 hour. Serve cold. May be kept in a sealed container up to 1 week.

PORK LOIN OVER A BED OF ROOT VEGETABLES

SERVES 6

3 parsnips, peeled and cut into 2-inch dice
1 turnip, peeled, cut into 1-inch dice
8 new or Yukon Gold potatoes, quartered
1 stalk celery, cut into 2-inch slices
5 shallots, halved
5 garlic cloves, peeled
⅓ cup olive oil

2 teaspoons plus 1 tablespoon salt
1 teaspoon plus ½ tablespoon pepper
1 4-pound pork loin, fat lightly scored
1 teaspoon ground cumin
1 teaspoon ground allspice
1 teaspoon ground cloves
2 tablespoons packed light brown sugar

Preheat the oven to 350°F.

In a large roasting pan, toss the parsnips, turnip, potatoes, celery, shallots, and garlic with the oil. Season with 2 teaspoons of the salt and 1 teaspoon of the pepper. Place the pork, fat side up, on top of the vegetables.

In a small bowl, combine the remaining 1 tablespoon salt, the remaining ½ tablespoon pepper, the cumin, allspice, cloves, and sugar. Rub the mixture on top of pork loin.

Roast until the pork registers 140° on an instant-read thermometer, about 30 minutes. If the vegetables are not quite fork-tender, transfer the pork to a platter and cover loosely with foil. Roast the vegetables until golden.

Slice the pork and serve over the vegetables.

BRAISED BRUSSELS SPROUTS WITH CREAM, BACON

SERVES 4

Brussels sprouts are such cute veggies. They look just like little cabbages. And, they are good for you too. It is, pardon the pun, sprouting up on menus everywhere. I like to lightly brown them, then braise them until just tender.

6 slices bacon
1 tablespoon butter
1½ pounds Brussels sprouts, stemmed
    and trimmed of any loose leaves
1 shallot, finely minced

¼ cup white wine
1½ cups chicken stock
¼ cup heavy cream
1 teaspoon allspice
Salt and pepper to taste

In a large sauté pan on medium heat, cook the bacon, turning frequently, until crisp. Remove the bacon from the pan, leaving the fat. Turn the heat to low and add the butter to the sauté pan. When the butter has melted, add the Brussels sprouts and increase the heat to high. Cook the Brussels sprouts, frequently shaking the pan and stirring, until light golden brown.

Turn the heat to medium low and add the shallot, cooking until just translucent, about 2 minutes. Add the wine and stock. Bring to a boil and reduce to a simmer. Cook for 10 minutes. Add the cream and allspice and simmer an additional 7 minutes or until just fork-tender, and the cream has thickened. Crumble the bacon into the mixture. Taste for seasoning.

Serve immediately.

BUTTERNUT SQUASH LASAGNA

SERVES 10

Oone day, a woman walked into my shop to ask me to cater a party. Not just any party, but a 12-course dinner pairing the best of her wine cellar with my food. I had never worked for her before, and she had never even tasted my cooking. Still, she hired me on the spot. I spent weeks happily tasting her wines and selecting the perfect food-friendly wines from her collection.

I fell in love with a Chardonnay that was bursting with the flavors of buttered popcorn and toasted hazelnut, so I created this lasagna to pair with it. It went on to become an iconic dish at Picnic. I can't tell you how many of these we have made, for good reason.

1 cup butter
1 large or 2 small butternut squash, peeled and cubed (about 5 cups)
½ cup chopped onion
1 cup chicken stock, plus more as needed
Salt and pepper to taste

8 ounces ricotta cheese
4 cups Béchamel Sauce (recipe follows)
10 ounces fresh lasagna noodles or fresh pasta sheets
¼ cup thinly sliced fresh sage leaves
¼ cup chopped toasted hazelnuts

In a large deep skillet, melt ¼ cup of the butter over medium heat. Add the squash and the onions. Sauté over medium high heat, stirring frequently for about 10 minutes. Add stock and cook, stirring and adding more stock as needed, for 30 to 45 minutes, until the squash softens and literally falls apart.

Raise the heat to high and bring to a boil until the stock evaporates. Add ¼ cup of butter, stir the squash, and cook for 10 minutes more, until the butter melts and the squash browns slightly. Season the squash with salt and pepper to taste. Turn off the heat and let cool. Once the squash is lukewarm, stir in the ricotta cheese.

While the squash is cooling, make the Béchamel Sauce. Preheat the oven to 350°F.

Spread ½ cup of the Béchamel Sauce in the bottom of a 9 x 13-inch baking dish. Top with a layer of noodles, ½ cup Béchamel Sauce, and a third of the squash mixture. Repeat two more times with noodles, Béchamel Sauce, and the squash mixture. Finish with 1 cup of Béchamel Sauce, spread evenly over the top. Reserve the remaining Béchamel sauce for reheating or for adding extra sauce to the plate.

Cover the lasagna with foil, and bake for 20 minutes. Remove the foil and bake for 20 to 30 minutes more, or until it begins to brown on top. Remove the lasagna from the oven and re-cover it with foil. Let rest for 15 minutes.

While the lasagna rests, in a skillet, melt the remaining ½ cup butter over low heat. Add the sage and cook and stir until the butter turns golden brown.

Cut the lasagna into squares. To serve, drizzle with sage browned butter, a drizzle of Béchamel Sauce, and sprinkle with the hazelnuts.

BÉCHAMEL SAUCE

4 cups whole milk
3 or 4 fresh sage leaves
½ cup butter
½ cup flour

1 teaspoon salt
½ teaspoon white pepper
¼ teaspoon ground nutmeg

In a medium saucepan, heat up the milk and sage over low heat. Heat the milk until hot, but do not let it come to a boil. Turn off the heat, and discard the sage.

In a large saucepan, melt the butter over medium heat. Add the flour and cook, whisking constantly, for 2 minutes. Add the milk and cook, whisking constantly, until the sauce thickens. Stir in the salt, white pepper, and nutmeg, and turn off the heat.

A NOTE on CHRISTMAS TABLECLOTHS

One of the spiffiest things to dress up the holiday table with is a Christmas tablecloth. My heirloom holiday tablecloth is white and red cotton. Sounds boring, but actually, when guests would arrive at the holidays, they were all asked to "autograph" the tablecloth because, as I told them, after the holidays, I would embroider their names onto it, for posterity. Sure enough, all those years later, when people come to the house during the holidays, they're always peeking at the cloth, looking for their name. If you don't know how to embroider, find a friend who can.

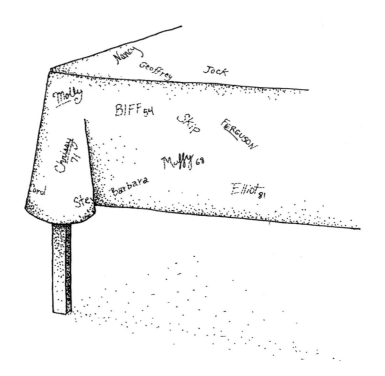

STANDING RIB ROAST WITH YORKSHIRE PUDDING

SERVES 6 GOOD EATERS

Every family has its own holiday traditions at the dinner table. Hams, turkeys, tenderloins of beef—but to me, nothing says Christmas more than a standing rib roast with Yorkshire pudding. Yorkshire pudding has been made in the north of England since the mid-1700s. If it has stayed this popular for centuries, there must be a reason.

The trick to a great rib roast is in the cut of meat itself. Order the first three ribs—they are the biggest, meatiest, and tastiest. If you're serving a crowd, ask your butcher for two roasts, using the first three ribs for both. It costs a bit more to purchase, but what better dinner to splurge on than Christmas?

As for doneness, I like to cook it to just above rare, because if guests want it cooked more it is easy enough to pop slices of the roast back into the oven with a little jus.

1 7-pound standing rib roast, cut from the first three bones
3 tablespoons plus 1 teaspoon salt
3 tablespoons pepper

3 eggs, beaten
1 cup whole milk
1 cup flour

Preheat the oven to 450°F.

Place the roast, fat side up, in a heavy-bottomed roasting pan that just fits the roast. Season generously on all sides with 3 tablespoons of the salt and the pepper. Roast for 15 minutes. Reduce the heat to 350°F and roast for about 1 hour more.

While the roast cooks, make the batter for the Yorkshire pudding. In a large bowl, whisk together the eggs and milk. Slowly whisk in the flour and the remaining 1 teaspoon salt. Cover and refrigerate until just before cooking.

Check the temperature of the roast with an instant-read thermometer. When the roast is 125°F, remove it from the oven and transfer it to a platter. Reserve the roast drippings.

Cover the roast loosely with foil and let rest while you make the Yorkshire pudding.

Raise the oven to 450°F. Adjust the oven rack to the lower third of the oven.

Pour off 3 tablespoons of fat from the roast drippings into a metal pie plate or cake pan and pop it into the oven for a couple of minutes until it's good and hot. Remove from the oven and pour the chilled batter into the hot pie plate. Bake in the lower third of the oven for 20 minutes, or until good and puffy.

Slice the roast and arrange on a platter.

Remove the Yorkshire pudding from pan and place around sliced roast. Serve.

PINECONE CHEESE BALL

SERVES ENOUGH FOR A FUN PARTY

A cheese ball shaped like a pinecone lights up a buffet table. Not to mention, it is a mighty tasty little bite. The cheese comes together in a jiffy, but creating the pinecone takes a bit of patience. Garnish it with rosemary or even a little sprig of fresh pine.

2 8-ounce packages cream cheese, softened
3 tablespoons Madras curry powder
1 teaspoon salt
1 5-ounce jar Major Grey's chutney

2 bunches scallions, thinly sliced
12 slices cooked bacon, crumbled
1 16-ounce can smoked almonds
1 sprig fresh rosemary or pine
Crackers, for serving

In a small bowl, combine the cheese, curry powder, and salt. Stir in the chutney, scallions, and bacon.

On a festive platter, shape the cheese into a pinecone form of your choice. Chill, and refrigerate for 1 hour. Carefully layer the almonds, pointed sides up, around the cheese ball.

Garnish with the rosemary. Serve with crackers.

ORNAMENT COLLECTIONS

We preps do collect some things. Nautical items, duck decoys, and antique salt cellars are common collections. In my family, we collect Christmas ornaments. Perhaps "collect" is the wrong word—amassed could be better. Growing up, there were boxes—old, disintegrating boxes—that simply said "special ornaments." These were put on the tree after the tree-trimming party had ended. The sturdiest top branches were reserved for these heirlooms.

The collection kept growing, as we added everything from cute Hallmark ornaments to the tackiest ornaments we could find on our travels. I won that competition with my Murano glass Santa on a gondola.

MRS. CLAUS'S CHRISTMAS PUNCH

SERVES A CROWD

The name of this punch makes me smile so much that I had to make it for my annual tree-trimming party. I admit, it was not very popular because, well, there is no alcohol in it. But I served it at a holiday lunch, and it was a big hit! I added the optional vodka for that one.

1 gallon apple cider
½ gallon orange juice
20 whole cloves

20 whole allspice
5 cinnamon sticks, broken in half
4 cups vodka (optional)

In an 8-quart pot, combine the cider, orange juice, cloves, allspice, and cinnamon and bring to a boil over high heat. Reduce the heat to low and simmer for 30 minutes. Strain. Discard the cloves, allspice, and cinnamon.

To make it a bit more interesting, add the vodka. Serve hot.

CHRISTMAS COCKTAIL

Bells on bobtails ring, keeping tension light . . .

It is wonderful to see family at the holidays; however due to the various mix of personalities that can result from both traditional and modern family combinations, all that getting together is often a bit stressful. My friend Kathy's family always serves this cocktail on Christmas Eve, as an icebreaker to the evening. It is a real holiday "spirit lifter."

There is nothing like a pitcher of cocktails, but this one is best made by the glass.

2 fluid ounces Mount Gay rum
3 fluid ounces orange juice

1 fluid ounce cranberry juice

Fill a double old-fashioned glass (preferably with Spode's Christmas Tree pattern) with ice. Add the rum and orange juice, and give it a stir. Dribble the cranberry juice into the glass for a festive look.

THE TREE-TRIMMING PARTY

I have hosted a tree-trimming party every year since my teens. I can't think of a faster, easier way to get a Christmas tree up while also enjoying a festive party with friends donned in their holiday finest. What other time can the ladies take out their little cashmere sweaters with embroidered poinsettias and the gentlemen bring out their Black Watch plaid pants coupled with a tacky Christmas tie embroidered with candy canes? Everyone is in the holiday spirit, and, more than likely, the evening will end with a caroling party, when everyone knocks on the neighbor's door and attempts to sing "We Wish You a Merry Christmas" in harmony.

Decorate the house for the party tastefully. Put a wreath on the door, and perhaps on the bay windows. Don the mantel with a garland of pine. Hang those hand-knitted or needlepointed stockings.

Take out the Christmas china and painted wineglasses that you got as a wedding gift and have never had the occasion to use. Use a festive tablecloth (see page 226) and set a bowl of the nicest ornaments from your collection as a centerpiece (so that after Biff has a few cocktails and decides it's time to hang ornaments, they will be safe from harm).

Put the rest of your ornaments in baskets, and place hooks in a bowl nearby, making it easy for the guests to do their job. After all, you are feeding them for one reason—to get your tree trimmed with a minimal amount of work. The timing on the following menu (page 234) is important. Over the years I have learned that once the buffet is out, the guests no longer lift a finger to decorate.

One more thing: the tree-trimming party is the one event of the year that I hire help. It is great to have three helpers, if budget permits—one who greets the guests and hangs their coats, cleans up dirty glasses and cocktail napkins; one in the kitchen to set out the buffet; and a bartender to keep the drinks flowing.

MENU

SNACKS AND APPETIZERS (set out before the guests arrive)

• **Bowl of potato chips, store-bought onion dip**

• **Original Chex Mix** (page 78)

• **Pinecone Cheese Ball** (page 229)

• **Classic Shrimp Cocktail with Tequila-Lime Sauce** (page 152) and herbed mayonnaise

• **Brie with Cranberry-Orange Relish** (page 212) spread on top, with a box of Triskets

• **Chicken Liver Pâté** (page 157) with baguette slices and green grapes

• **Deviled Eggs** (page 164)

• **Store-bought pigs in a blanket** (the frozen kosher ones are the best)

• **Spinach dip** (brought by a friend) in a brown-bread bowl

• **Quintessential Crab Dip** (page 167) with club crackers

ON THE BUFFET (do not set out the buffet food until the tree
is three quarters of the way decorated)

• **Glazed Spiral Ham** (page 201)

• **Peg Day's Baked Beans** (page 61)

• **Green bean casserole**

• **Harvard Beets** (page 87)

• **Warm German Potato Salad** (page 102)

• **Roasted tenderloin of beef**

• **Assorted tea sandwiches**, such as cream cheese and maraschino cherry, egg,
tuna, ham (for ideas, see page 196)

DESSERT

Friends will show up with cookies as hostess gifts. Serve them. Done.

THE CHRISTMAS TREE

Most preps I know would never, ever have a tree professionally "decorated." Nor should there be a theme tree as the main tree in the house. The caveat to that is, of course, the fund-raiser tree that one would get at, say, a Junior League holiday auction. These trees, traditionally of the tabletop variety, usually have a cute theme. Lilly Pulitzer colors, country cabin, and beaches are all de rigueur. Keep them in the guest room, the den, the bay window, or wherever you like.

However, decorate a tree—a real tree, in a real stand, with real ornaments. The ornaments should be eclectic. It is fine to hang your grandmother's silver bell next to a Hallmark-style ornament. Alma mater ornaments, cute little mice, and ornaments collected on trips are all appropriate.

The lights should be colored, and by no means should they blink. More than likely, someone will spend hours trying to find the reason why half the sets of lights just won't light. But eventually, after a few cocktails and lots of complaining, the lights will festively set the stage for the ornaments. Do get someone else to do that job, and remind them to hide all the wires.

Garland and tinsel are a no. The tree can be topped with a star (that is not lit or blinking in any manner), an angel, or with a decoration made by your child ten years ago. A little model sailboat or a starfish works well, too.

Preferably, the tree should go up two days before your party—one day to let it open up and a second day to have someone (who you have had to coerce) do the lights. Try to put the tree up Christmas week so it is in its true glory on the Big Day. Take it down on January 6 (the twelfth day of Christmas).

A PAIR OF CHRISTMAS COOKIES

I always knew the holidays had arrived the day after Thanksgiving, when my mother would make the first of many trips to the grocery store for her cookie ingredients. Pounds and pounds of flour, granulated sugar, brown sugar, and candied fruits sprouted up like weeds in the pantry. The fridge was always filled with cream cheese, butter, and eggs.

My mom would start making Christmas cookies on December 1 and would make them pretty much every night right up until Christmas Eve. Dozens of tins of cookies were stacked in the dining room, waiting to become what was all of our neighbors', friends', and family's favorite Christmas present: a plate of her signature Christmas cookies. If you were a close friend or relative, she would put them on a festive Christmas plate, perhaps Wedgewood. The neighbors, bridge club members, and schoolteachers got them on a nice big paper plate. They were all packaged up and ready to go Christmas Eve morning.

My job was to use a little antique nut chopper and chop the nuts. In return I was allowed to watch television as I worked. I can't even begin to think of how many pounds of nuts I ran through the chopper.

Here I share her most requested cookies, the nut roll and walnut balls. A friend recently said they were perhaps the best cookies she had ever sampled. Make them, at least once, and see for yourself.

WALNUT BALLS

MAKES 48 COOKIES

1 cup butter
¼ cup granulated sugar
2 teaspoons vanilla extract

2 cups flour
2 cups finely chopped walnuts
1 cup confectioners' sugar

Preheat the oven to 300°F.

Using a standing mixer fitted with the paddle attachment, beat the butter and granulated sugar on high speed until almost white in color. Add the vanilla and beat until combined.

With the mixer on low, add the flour, a little at a time, and beat until combined. Fold in in walnuts. Roll into ¾-inch balls and place on an ungreased baking sheet.

Bake for 30 to 35 minutes. While the cookies are baking, spread the confectioners' sugar on a plate. Remove the cookies from the oven and roll immediately in confectioners' sugar.

Transfer to a wire rack to let cool, then roll again in confectioners' sugar.

NUT ROLLS

MAKES 64 COOKIES

FOR THE NUT FILLING
2 egg whites
1½ cups finely chopped walnuts
1 cup sugar
1 teaspoon vanilla extract

FOR THE PASTRY
1 cup (2 sticks) butter, softened
1 8-ounce package cream cheese,
   softened
2 egg yolks
1 teaspoon vanilla extract
3 cups flour

For the nut filling: In a medium bowl, whisk the egg whites until they become frothy. Stir in the walnuts, sugar, and vanilla.

Preheat the oven to 375°F. Line a baking sheet with parchment paper.

For the pastry: Using a standing mixer fitted with the paddle attachment, beat the butter and cream cheese on high speed until fluffy. With the mixer on low, add the eggs yolks and vanilla and beat until combined.

With the mixer on low, add the flour, a little at a time, and beat until a soft dough forms. Turn the dough onto a floured work surface, and divide it into 4 pieces. Roll each piece into a ball.

Roll out 1 dough ball into a 12-inch circle. Spread one quarter of the nut filling evenly onto the circle. Using a sharp knife, cut the circle, pizza style, into 16 wedges.

Working from the outside in, roll each wedge up until it resembles a scroll. Place the rolls on the prepared baking sheet. Bake for 15 minutes, or until golden.

Repeat with the remaining dough and nut filling.

HOT BUTTERED RUM

SERVES 4

This drink is perfect for après-ski, or as a warm-up after any winter activity, even shoveling the driveway. The butter needs to be made a day in advance, so if the forecast calls for snow, think ahead and get started.

FOR THE SPICED BUTTER
½ **cup butter, softened**
¼ **cup packed light brown sugar**
1 **teaspoon ground cinnamon**
½ **teaspoon ground allspice**
½ **teaspoon ground nutmeg**

2 **teaspoons orange zest**

FOR THE HOT BUTTERED RUM
8 **fluid ounces dark rum**
3 **cups boiling water**
1 **orange, cut into 4 wedges**

For the spiced butter: Using a standing mixer fitted with the paddle attachment, beat the sugar with the butter, cinnamon, allspice, nutmeg and orange zest until it is combined. Transfer the spiced butter onto a sheet of plastic wrap and roll the plastic around the butter, forming a log. Twist the ends of the plastic to seal. Freeze overnight.

For the drink: Pour 2 fluid ounces of the rum into each of four heatproof mugs and top with ¾ cup of the boiling water. Squeeze the juice from 1 orange wedge into each mug and top with a pat of frozen spiced butter. Serve immediately.

Note: You will have some leftover butter on hand for the next storm. Keep it in the freezer for up to three months, or until spring arrives.

THE
PREPPY
KITCHEN

A WELL "STOCKED" FRIDGE

I have to say, if you want to impress your guests and family with your cooking savvy and you want to make a dish as good as the one you had at that four-star restaurant in Manhattan (or wherever), the key is to keep stock on hand. The nice thing about homemade stock is that it contains no salt at all.

Spend one day making a couple of stocks, and store them in the freezer, in ice cube trays as many recommend. It is a darned good idea, I must say. Stocks are simple, but veal stock is very time-consuming. If you cannot get veal bones, go ahead and make beef stock. But I think you will find that veal stock is a much better use of your time. It is rich and wonderful.

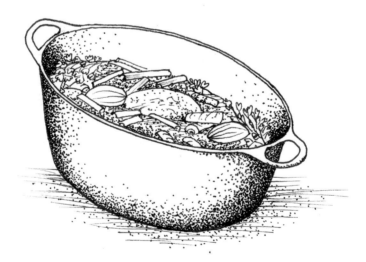

CHEATER'S ROASTED CHICKEN STOCK

MAKES APPROXIMATELY 2 QUARTS

2 store-bought roasted chickens
1 large onion, quartered
4 stalks celery, cut into large dice
4 carrots, cut into large dice

3 bay leaves
4 sprigs fresh parsley
5 whole black peppercorns
3 quarts cold water

In a large stockpot, add the chicken, onion, celery, carrots, bay leaves, parsley, and peppercorns, and cover with the cold water. Bring to a boil over very high heat. Reduce the heat to medium and simmer for 3½ hours. You will notice some grayish gunk that will rise to the top. Using a ladle, skim that off every 30 minutes.

Strain the stock through a fine-mesh strainer. Return the stock back to the pot, and cook over low heat about 3 hours, until reduced by a third.

Fill a sink with ice. Transfer the pot to the sink to cool, then refrigerate overnight. The next day, ladle the stock into ice cube trays and freeze up to 3 months.

VEAL STOCK

MAKES ABOUT 3 QUARTS

8 pounds veal bones, cut into 3- to
   4-inch pieces
¼ cup vegetable oil
2 large onions, quartered
4 stalks celery, chopped
4 carrots, chopped

½ cup tomato paste
2 gallons cold water
3 bay leaves
8 sprigs fresh parsley
10 whole black peppercorns

Preheat the oven to 475°F.

Put the bones in a large roasting pan, making sure they are in a single layer. Add the oil and toss until lightly coated. Roast for about 45 minutes, turning every 15 minutes or so, until browned.

Transfer the bones to a 3-gallon stockpot. Drain off half of the fat from the roasting pan, leaving being any browned bits of meat in the pan. Place the roasting pan over two burners on medium heat, and add the onions, celery, and carrots. Cook until the vegetables begin to turn golden brown, being careful not to scorch the pan. Add the tomato paste and toss to coat the vegetables, cooking about 5 to 10 minutes, until the paste turns a rust color.

Transfer the vegetable mixture to the stockpot and cover with the cold water. Bring to a boil over very high heat. Reduce the heat to medium and simmer for 10 hours (yes, 10 hours). You will notice some grayish gunk that will rise to the top. Using a ladle, skim that off every 30 minutes. Check the liquid level and add more water as needed to ensure the bones are fully covered.

Fill a sink with ice. When the stock has simmered the full 10 hours, strain it through a fine-mesh strainer into another large pot. Transfer the pot to the sink to cool, then refrigerate overnight.

The next day, bring the stock to a boil over high heat. Reduce the heat to medium and simmer for 2 to 3 hours, until reduced by half. Fill a sink with ice. Transfer the pot to the sink to cool, once again. Ladle the stock into ice cube trays or small containers and freeze up to 3 months. Pat yourself on the back for having the patience to do this. Trust me, you will be rewarded.

NOW, OF COURSE, ON TO THE OTHER IMPORTANT ITEMS: A WELL-STOCKED BAR

I like to keep enough liquor on hand to accommodate nearly every taste, but not so much that the bottles sit getting dusty and crusty. All the liqueurs and spirits should be top shelf.

SPIRITS
Gin
Vodka
Scotch
Bourbon
Rye
Dark Rum
Tequila
Vermouth

LIQUEURS
Green crème de menthe
Chambord
Grand Marnier
Brandy
Crème de cacao

MIXERS
Cranberry juice
Tonic water
Pineapple juice
Orange juice
Grapefruit juice
Clamato or V8
Seltzer
Ginger beer

GARNISHES
Olives
Lemons
Limes
Oranges
Cocktail onions
Maraschino cherries

OTHER
Tabasco sauce
Bitters
Prepared horseradish
Swizzle sticks

THE PREPPY PANTRY

It is easier to put together a meal when you have everything except the fresh products on hand. And it's nice to know that if you have an impromptu get-together, you can pretty much pull off cooking a meal.

IN THE FRIDGE
- Olives
- A few nice cheeses
- Lemons and limes
- Butter
- Package of smoked salmon
- Ham steak
- Bacon
- Heavy cream
- Dijon mustard
- Mayo
- Ketchup
- Eggs
- Capers
- Cocktail sauce
- Prepared horseradish
- Orange juice
- Grapefruit juice
- Sour cream
- Box of baking soda, open (You may be tempted to use it for baking, but don't! It won't be right after sitting in the fridge. Believe me, I know from experience.)
- Celery
- Carrots
- Cold pack port wine cheese

IN THE FREEZER
- Stocks (pages 247 and 248)
- Pint of ice cream
- Plenty of ice (cocktails!)
- Extra pound of butter
- Puff pastry
- Bag of shrimp
- Breakfast sausages
- Frozen pigs in a blanket
- English muffins
- Eileen's Crabbies (page 19)

IN THE ACTUAL PANTRY
- Flour
- Sugar, white and light brown
- Bisquick or other biscuit mix
- Triskets and Wheat Thins
- Chips
- Assorted condensed soups
- Tomato paste
- Canned pineapple
- Seasoned bread crumbs
- Panko bread crumbs
- Anchovies
- Marinated sun-dried tomatoes
- Vegetable oil
- Olive oil

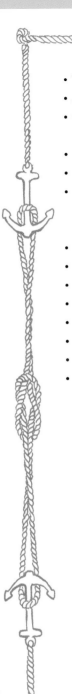

- Worcestershire sauce
- Jell-O (assorted flavors)
- Canned oil-packed tuna fish (only white meat)
- English breakfast tea
- Soy sauce
- Assorted vinegars, such as tarragon, champagne, cider, balsamic, white (for dyeing Easter eggs)
- Canned string beans
- Elbow macaroni
- Spaghetti or vermicelli
- Jarred chipped beef
- Extra jar of mayo
- Dry onion soup mix (dip on hand!)
- Honey
- Assorted nuts, such as walnuts, pecans, smoked almonds

SPICES AND SUCH

Unless you plan to do a lot of cooking, it is best to buy small containers of spices and replace them every six months or so. A lot of flavor disappears as these spices and herbs age in the jar.

- Allspice
- Bay leaves
- Bell's Seasoning
- Cayenne pepper
- Chili powder
- Ground cinnamon and cinnamon sticks
- Cloves, whole and ground
- Ground cumin
- Ground ginger
- Kosher salt
- Madras curry powder
- Nutmeg, whole and ground
- Old Bay
- Paprika
- Peppers, black and white
- Sage
- Seasoned salt
- Table salt
- Tarragon
- Thyme

ACKNOWLEDGMENTS

A well-deserved cheers to:

First, to my crackerjack editor, Katie Salisbury, who kept her sense of humor and style while attending photo shoots, finding the perfect illustrator, and immersing herself in the lifestyle to the point that she is now an honorary prep.

Here's to my agent, David Larabell of the David Black Agency who, within ten minutes of reading my proposal, called and said we've got a book! Speaking of which, special thanks to Sue Huffman and Zanne Stewart for introducing me to him.

Gee, it was so very kind of Sara Moulton, a preppy and one of the most talented chefs around, to write such a lovely introduction.

Ted Axelrod did a brilliant job with capturing the feel of the food with his gorgeous and playful photography. Now, have a beer.

Also, to Kathy Bresnan—without her support, I couldn't be bothered—and to Sally Hassebroek Merchant, who insisted I write this book to begin with. Thanks, ladies!

My long (and I do mean long) time friend Steven Kopf, spent hours and hours helping me see the project through. Annabel Schlair, who had the faith in me to partner on our Picnic. Gretchen Viggiano, who was supportive from the get-go, and always took the late-night frustrated calls and packed me with great ideas, not to mention the perfect needlepoint belt.

My cousin Betsy graciously went through hundreds of her mother's recipes looking for the ones that I wanted for the book. And, my "sis" Nan did the same.

To Lorraine Mullica Ash, who got me my start in journalism and writing by telling me I had a unique voice.

To Jacqueline and Bill Willis, Rita Cookson (pastry chef extraordinaire), Nicole Grace, Rachel Perlow, Sharyn Roesler, Aleece Nolan, Heather Bean, and Janet and Gary Montroy who tested recipes and provided much needed feedback. And to Ellyn Komito-Casey and Babs Wilkins for hanging out at the many photo shoots, offering to do whatever needed to get done. And to Gerry Gould for the great insight.

Thanks, too, to Susanne Lovisolo, Nancy Nolte, and Buffy McKay for sharing their gorgeous homes for photography shoots. Lindsey Gamble of Elegantly Iced Cakes made the perfect preppy shower cake for the photos.

To the ladies of the Junior League of Bergen County. Your support has always been key to my career. A special hats off to Peg Knight and Trudy Dial, two of the most remarkable League ladies ever.

Sherry Kahn, Stu is here in spirit, reminding me of the wonderful catering advice you both gave me: "Your people drink, then eat enough to absorb alcohol. Cook half the food and serve twice the drinks. For our people, double the food and half the liquor." True words, indeed!

Joan Ash, I wish you were around to see this.

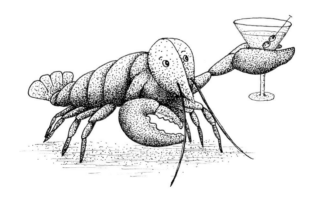

INDEX